LO SHU GRID NUMEROLOGY

SECRET LIFE PREDICTION METHOD

SUMIT KUMAR

Made with ♥ on the Notion Press Platform
www.notionpress.com

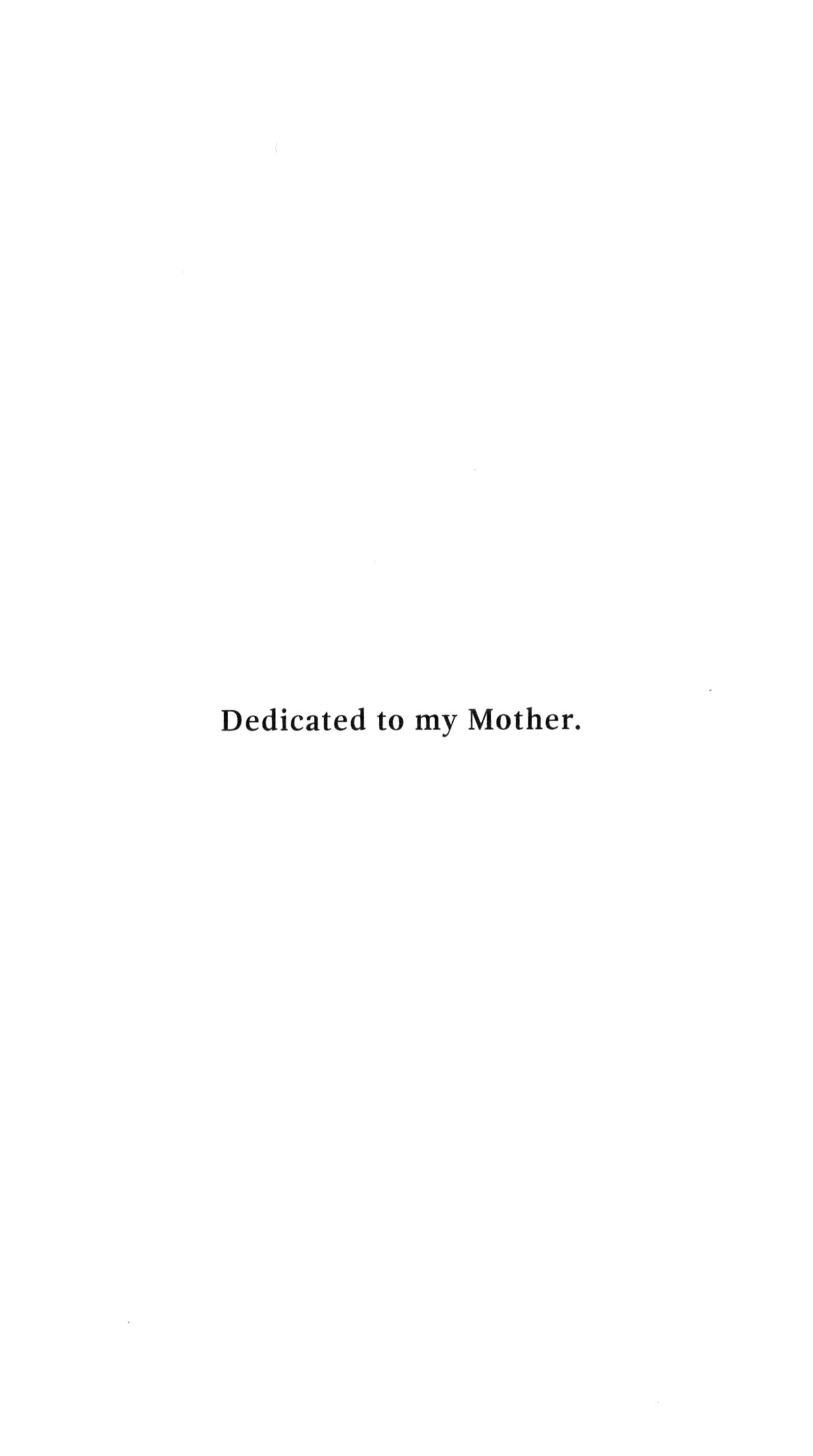

Dedicated to my Mother.

Contents

Preface

Numerology is an ancient study that draws meaning from different numbers, number combinations, letters, and symbols in your life. This art can help us tap into the underlying patterns of the universe and reveal new truths about who we are.

There are many ways in which numerology is read and understood. The evolution in the studies have created many branches depending upon the region, places, relevance. Lo Shu Grid numerology is one of that kind. Originated in China it has connection with indian system in form of Laxmi yantra.

The Purpose of this book is to give you an introductory knowledge and basic predictions possible in Lo Shu grid numerology. People who are masters in the field of numerology do say that numerology in itself is not a 100 % accurate science, it may vary for different individuals. But overall in comparison to Astrology and other methods, it is one of the easiest to learn and apply. When applied with full knowledge of astrology and other prediction methods numerology gives the best result.

The scope of this book is to give best possible understanding of this Chinese method and covers the basics of Lo Shu grid essential to understand the advance part in numerology. The book also covers the predictions in the area of marriage, marriage success/failure, Career, Finance , Stock Market , Career Fields, financial success etc. Case Study of prominent personalities are also included to make the understanding simple. At the end, the remedies related to it are provided in detail.

Lo Shu is very interesting numerological method and can be understood without any prior knowledge of any other predictive methods. One can draw their own chart and see through the problem areas and their possible solution.

This book will surely be fun for people who like to dive into mysticism. With this hope i would conclude and wish you have a great time with this knowledge.

Disclaimer : In the Case study the Birth dates taken for study are from the public domain and we expect that to be true for all the eminent personalities. Any mismatch of any sort is not in the purview of the responsibility of this book.

"Man can do what he wills but Man cannot will what he wills. If you understand the Language, the Numbers speak to you."

CHAPTER ONE

WHAT IS A LO SHU GRID ?

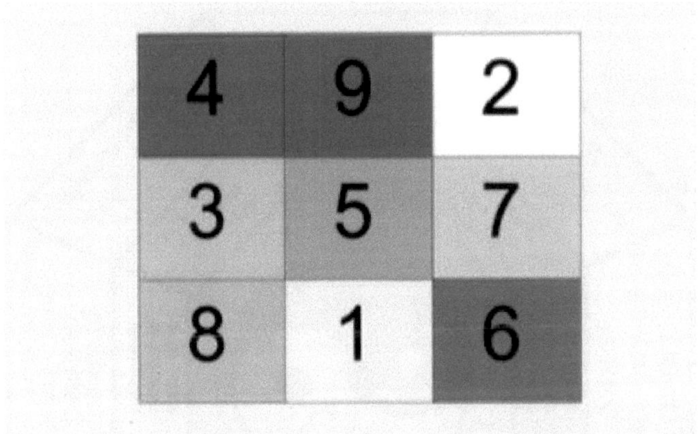

Lo Shu grid is a square-shaped design which consists of 9 numbers from 1 to 9 with 3 rows and 3 columns. It is called the magical grid because the total of each row and each column sums to 15. It is considered a sacred square. Chinese numerology has always been associated with the

Magical Lo Shu Grid, which was discovered around 4000 years ago. The intrinsic patterns of the base chart, together with the way the numbers move about the grid, are believed to offer clues on the characteristics and outcomes of events within the environment. The Lo Shu grid is the central principle behind "Flying Star Feng Shui" and also used in the interpretation of individual birth charts.

This diagram shown is a special magic square. It has been formulated after an intense research for creating a unique blend of ancient wisdom and modern science. It is the commitment to material and spiritual prosperity of today's man that has led to designing this simple and logical yet effective technique.

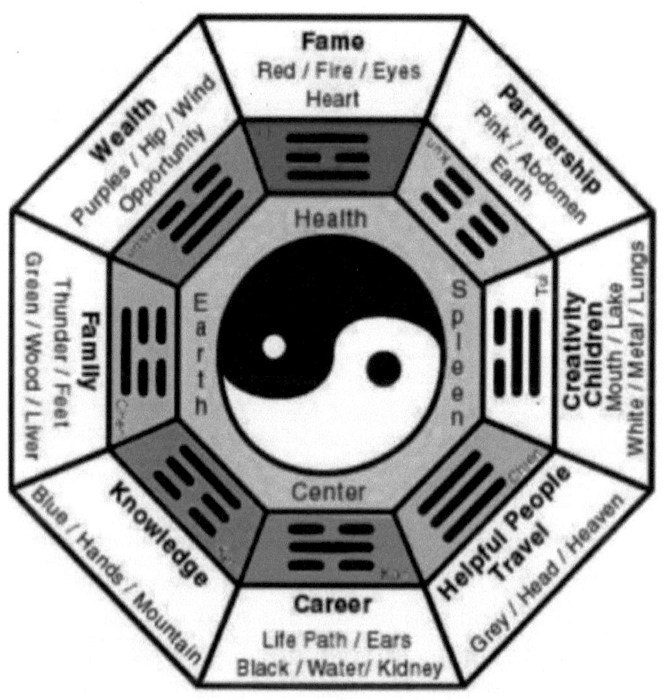

The story of this square's origin dates back to almost 4000 years old China. Legend says that Chinese people found a tortoise shell during the flood of the river Luo.

This tortoise-shell had a 3×3 square on its back and the sum of every horizontal, vertical, and diagonal row was added up to 15. Now 15 is the number of days between the new moon and the full moon. Number 5 was also highly regarded in ancient China and this magic square had a number 5 in the center.

In those ancient times in China it was considered auspicious because they believed that God lived inside tortoise and turtle shells.

The diagram above illustrates the relationship between the eight-sided Pa-Kua and the nine grids of Lo-Shu magic square. Please note that the Pa-Kua shown here places the direction of South at the top, to correspond with the number 9. This is because the Chinese compass places South at the top, and to ensure consistency and accuracy, it is necessary when relationships between symbols are being analyzed, and to comply with the practice followed in the ancient manuals.

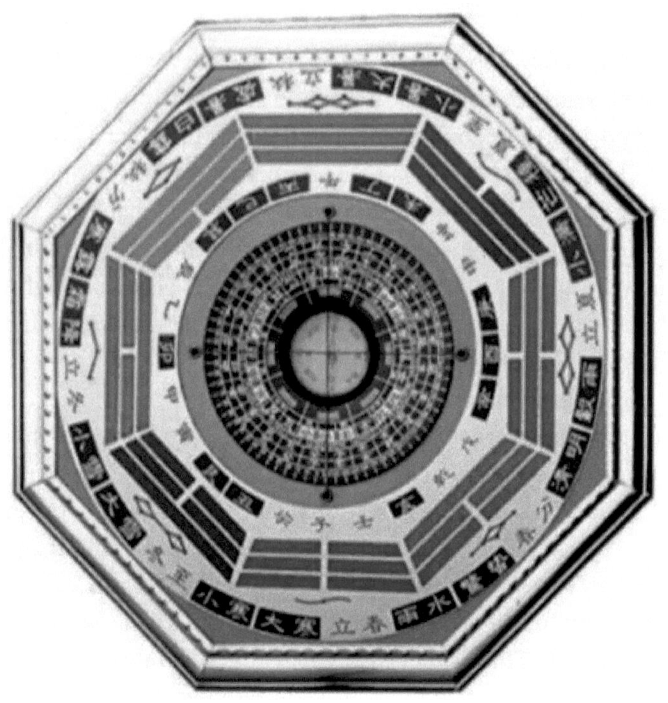

For practical purposes, however, you may use modern compasses, which place North at the top. However, it is vital that mistakes should not be made while attempting to conceive interpretation based on symbolic relationship between numbers and the Trigrams.

An ancient form of divination, Chinese numerology dates back about 4,000 years. The birth of this art form is retold in the Legend of the Turtle

Between 2205 and 2198 B.C.E. He had a reputation of being wise and ruled in a just manner.

At one time Emperor Yu was engaged in the supervision of building a dam on the Yellow River. Sitting by the bank of the river he was interrupted by a divine turtle which appeared from the river. The name of the turtle was Hi.

The emperor was astonished when he took a closer look at the back of the Turtle. There was a magic square, nine numbers in all. The numbers added up to 15 in every direction.

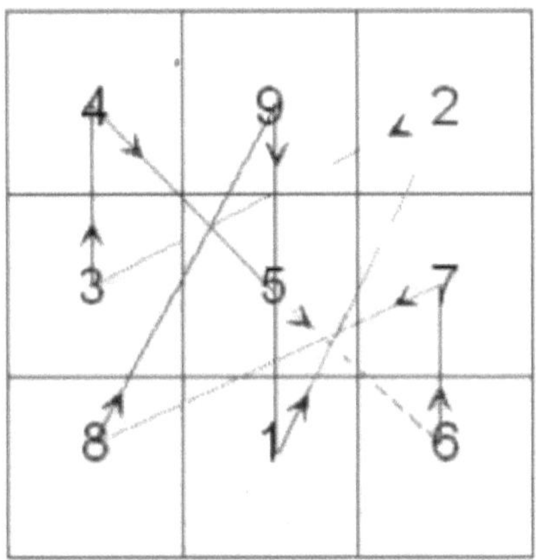

Emperor Yu is widely acknowledged as the one who first discovered the magic square, brought to him on the shell of the turtle, which aside from being an omen of good luck in Chinese lore, is well known for its divine wisdom.

This magic square is known as the "Lo Shu" square and is important in all forms of Chinese spirituality surrounding numbers such as Feng Shui, the Ki Star theory, and The Chinese Zodiac. Chinese numerology readings are based on mystical traditions, including the I-Ching - which is sometimes also used for numerology compatibility readings. Over time Chinese numerology has evolved into three different systems that are being used today. There is the Western version of Chinese numerology, the traditional Chinese numerology and the Ki system. Whatever the method, the basic principles are the same in the modality.

Yang Numbers:

Examples of a 'yang number' are the 'odd numbers': 1, 3, 5, 7, 9, 11, etc.

Yin Numbers:

Examples of a 'yin number' are the 'even numbers': 2, 4, 6, 8, 10, 12, etc.

The Yin and Yang must be balanced. Yin and Yang are complementary and inseparable. It seems impossible to imagine one without the other. So if at any moment Yin is too strong Yang will be in the future and seek balance.

	Yin	Yang
Number	Even 2, 4, 6, 8	Odd 1, 3, 5, 7, 9
Position	Bottom	Top
Time	Night	Day
Season	Autumn, Winter	Spring, Summer
Direction	North, West	South, East
Element	Water	Fire
Gender	Female	Male
Heat	Cold	Hot
Humidity	Wet	Dry
Brightness	Dark	Light
Color	Black	White
Planet	Moon	Sun
View	Invisible	Visible
Planet	Earth	Heaven

Yin & Yang

Lucky Numbers:

A 'lucky number' is a number which is based on Chinese words that sound similar to other Chinese words. The numbers ‘6’, ‘8’, and ‘9“ are believed to have auspicious meanings because their names sound similar to words that have positive meanings. For example: Number ’8‘ is a lucky number because it sounds like ’prosperous‘ (in Cantonese language).

Unlucky Numbers:

Number ’4‘ and number ’13‘ are an ’unlucky number‘ according to the principles of Chinese numerology. The number ’13‘ adds up to ’4‘. The number ’4‘ sounds like the word 'death’ (in Cantonese language). One should notice here that you do not have to worry much about the number ‘4’ if the pronunciation of this number in your language does not sound similar to the word 'death'.

These principles can be applied to everything in life from auspicious dates such as your birthday, the date you conceived a child, or your wedding day to the colours you should paint your bedroom, investment tips in the stock market, and grades in school. Using the Lo Shu grid can give you great insights to the numbers in your life.

Note that the arrangement of the eight Trigram in this PaKua is based on the later Heaven Sequence. This is because all latter day practice of both Chinese Astrology and Chinese Feng Shui adopt this sequential representation of the Pa-Kua’s Trigrams.

CHAPTER TWO

LO SHU GRID PLANES

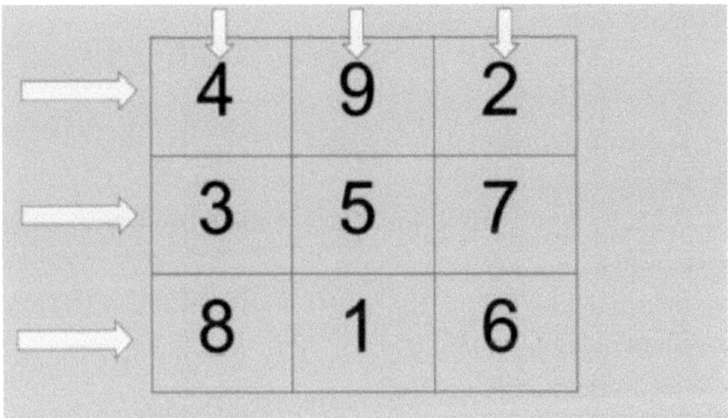

In the Lo Shu grid 6 straight planes are formed along with 2 diagonal planes. Each plane holds some significance and reflects the characteristics of a person. Presence of any plane shows the complete flow of energy without any obstructions. The person in that case has the natural ability related to that plane.

3 Horizontal Lo Shu Planes

Top row (4,9 and 2)

- It is called the Mental Plane.
- Represents the head of a person.
- Includes thinking, creating, imagining and analysing. People with this plane are
- very intelligent, have good creative ability.

Middle row (3, 5 and 7)

- It is called the Emotional Plane.
- Represents the body.
- Includes spirituality, intuition, feelings, and emotions. These people are very
- helpful, understand the pain of others and stand by them in good or bad times.

Bottom row (8, 1 and 6)

- It is called the Practical Plane.
- Represents the feet.
- Includes physical labor, creativity, and the ability to be practical in everyday life.

- These people are very hardworking, nothing comes easy to them, they earn their place in society through hard work.

Because of this they are very practical and do get easily influenced by others, taking their own decisions using their knowledge and experience. To use the head-legs analogy again, the feet are firmly placed on the ground in the Practical Plane.

Similarly, the vertical rows are also interpreted as follows:

3 Vertical Lo Shu Planes

First Column (4, 3 and 8)

- It is called the Thought Plane.
- Reveals the person's ability to come up with ideas, create things and carry them
- through to fruition.
- This is a plane of planner, visionary who can see things that nobody else can.
- Politicians and investors have this kind of plane. They see the opportunities when others can't.

Middle Column (9, 5 and 1)

- It is called the Will Plane.
- Gives determination and persistence to succeed.

- People with this plane have the strong will to do the necessary against all odds.
- Pushing the limits mentally physically comes from this plane.

Last Column (2, 7 and 6)

- It is called the Action Plane.
- Shows the person's ability to put his thoughts into action.
- Every plan and thought only remains in the head until the action is taken in the real world. These people are action takers.
- They just do it without much thought. Most of the time it pays off and sometimes it backfires.
- People from the sports field, Film stars generally have this plane present in their Lo Shu chart.

The three vertical rows make a natural progression. First of all, the person has to come up with an idea (Thought plane). He (or she) has to have determination and persistence (Will plane), otherwise the idea will never be acted upon.

The planning is done at this stage. Finally, the person needs to be able to put the idea and the determination into action (Action plane).

Other than those planes there are two more diagonal lanes which are very important. These will be discussed in the later part of this book. Both these planes are indicators of Finance, property and marriage.

CHAPTER THREE

DIRECTIONS & ELEMENTS

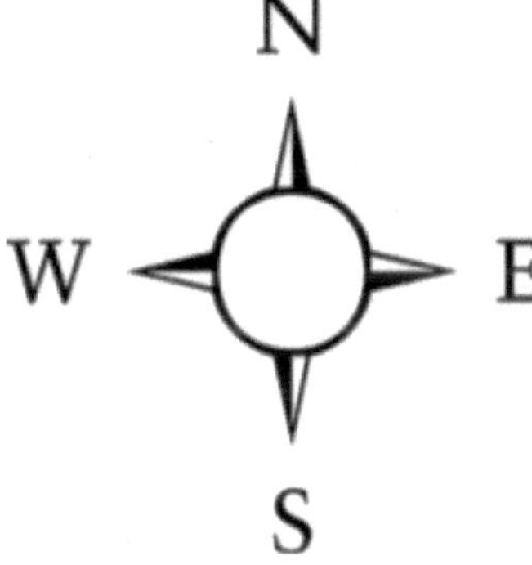

Each side and corner of a Loshu grid represents a certain direction as represented in the figure below.

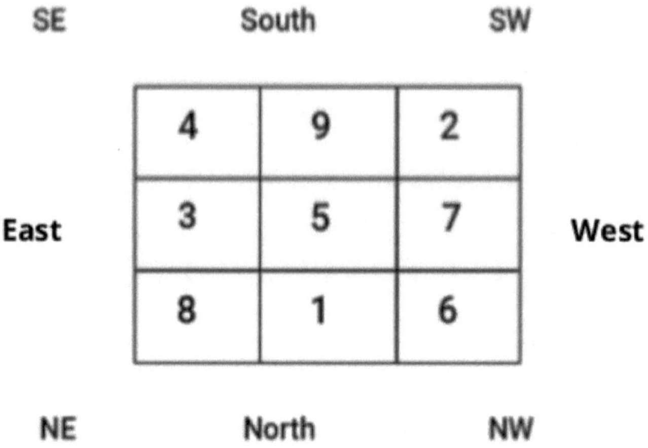

SE	South	SW
4	9	2
3	5	7
8	1	6
NE	North	NW

East | West

Directions

Each side represents certain directions so other than Number 5 all the numbers represent a certain direction.

Numbers	Direction
1	North
2	North-West
3	East
4	South-East
5	Centre
6	North-West
7	West
8	North- East
9	South

There are 5 fundamental elements in the Chinese system.

1. Fire
2. Water
3. Earth
4. Metal
5. Wood

Each of these elements and their characteristics are present in the numbers it represents. The Table below shows which number represents which elements.

Elements	Numbers
Fire	8
Water	1
Earth	2,5,8
Metal	7,6
Wood	4,3

Elements and respective Loshu Numbers

Directions and Elements are important to learn as these things help when it comes to assessing the problem areas and remedies related to those problems. Remedies are covered in later chapters of this book. To understand it briefly, let us assume there is a number 7 & 6 missing in any chart. That means the person is finding problems in finance and not getting support from friends. As per the chart above he is missing the metal element completely so he has to do the remedies related to it in the west or Northwest direction of the house or workplace.

Which Chinese Element Are You?

Chinese astrology differs from Western astrology in the fact that there are five elements in the Chinese system, and they emphasize different positions in life rather than a specific set of characteristics. However, these elements can still indicate the characteristics a person bears, and which traits someone from one element shares with others from the same element.

Five Chinese Elements

Element	Color	Symbol	Season	Day	Planet
Wood	Blue	Dragon	Spring	Thursday	Jupiter
Fire	Red	Phoenix	Summer	Tuesday	Mars
Earth	Yellow	Cauldron	Late Summer	Saturday	Saturn
Metal	White	Tiger	Autumn	Friday	Venus
Water	Black	Turtle	Winter	Wednesday	Mercury

There are five Chinese elements: wood, fire, earth, metal, and water. Each element is strongly related to one another, and there are many mnemonic devices to help remember them, such as:

- Wood feeds a fire
- Fire makes ash (earth)
- Earth contains metal
- Metal holds water (as in a pail or bucket)
- Water breeds wood

A few examples of how to interpret this include:

- Creation: Water gives life to Wood. Wood gives life to Fire. Fire gives life to Earth (ash). Earth gives life to Metal. Metal gives life to Water.
- Destruction: Wood's roots separate and break open the Earth. Earth absorbs Water. Water smothers Fire. Fire melts Metal. Metal penetrates Wood.

Much like the popular Yin-Yang symbol of Chinese astrology uses opposing force to promote the flow of energy, the five Chinese elements act in tandem, relate to one another, dance with one another, have specific attributes that separate one from the other, yet each depends on all the others to give it life.

Your Element

Your element is determined by the year of your birth. Therefore, it's easy to figure out your element. Just look at the last number in your birth year and match it to the element listed for that number.

- If the last number in your birth year is 0 or 1, your element is Metal
- If the last number in your birth year is 2 or 3, your element is Water.
- If the last number in your birth year is 4 or 5, your element is Wood.
- If the last number in your birth year is 6 or 7, your element is Fire.
- If the last number in your birth year is 8 or 9, your element is Earth.
- As an example, if you were born in 1989, your element would be Earth.

CHAPTER FOUR

Calculations of Lo Shu Chart

The most important and the only thing required to draw a Lo Shu Grid is the Date of birth (DOB) of that person. Unlike astrology where time and place of birth also matters, here only the correct date of birth does the trick.

Now Let us understand it by taking some examples.

Example 1

Let us suppose the DOB under the consideration is 12 July 1975

First step is to convert everything into numerical numbers i.e. 12-7-1975

Now the second step is to calculate the driver and conductor number. Driver number is the sum of the date in the date of birth. In this case the date is 12, so 1+2 = 3

Driver Number = 3

Conductor Number is the sum(addition) of all the numbers in date of birth (date, month & year). In the above case the addition comes out to be 1+2+7+1+9+7+5 =32 Now 32 has to be further added to come to a single digit, so 3+2=5

Conductor Number = 5

Now all the numbers are available to draw the Lo Shu grid for that person with this Date of birth.

Now place all the numbers available in the date of birth along with driver and conductor numbers derived out of it into the Lo Shu grid.

Note: All the numbers will come at their respective places in the grid.

Available Numbers are- 1 (twice), 2, 3 (driver number), 5(twice with conductor number), 7, 9

Lo Shu Grid for 12 July 1975 looks like this-

	9	2
3	55	7
	11	

Example 2

Date of Birth - 23 Nov 2007 = 23-11-2007

Driver number: 2+3 = 5

Conductor Number: 2+3+1+1+2+0+0+7 = 16 = 1+6 = 7

Now place all the numbers at their respective places

		22
3	5	7
	11	

Example 3

Date of Birth - 08 Feb 1991 = 08-02-1991

Driver number: 0+8 = 8

Conductor Number: 0+8+0+2+1+9+9+1 = 30 = 3+0 = 3

Now place all the numbers at their respective places.

	99	2
3		
88	11	

Note- Best practice is to write all the numbers in date of birth first then write the drive and conductor number in the grid so that you do not miss any number

CHAPTER FIVE

NUMBERS AND THEIR IMPACT

Southeast	South	Southwest
4 Wood Wealth Oldest Daughter	9 Fire Fame Middle Daughter	2 Earth Relationships Mom, Matriarch
East 3 Wood Health Oldest Son	**Center** 5 Earth Well-Being Family	**West** 7 Metal Kids Youngest Daughter
Northeast 8 Earth Knowledge Youngest Son	**North** 1 Water Career & Business Middle Son	**Northwest** 6 Metal Helpful People Dad, Patriarch

- Number 1 (COMMUNICATION): It is associated with communication. It relates how an individual reacts and communicates with others.
- Number 2 (SENSITIVE & INTUITION): It is associated with sensitive & intuition power. It relates how sensitive and intuitive an individual is.
- Number 3 (PLANNING & IMAGINATION): It relates the intellectual capacity of an individual, and the memory and ability to think clearly and logically.
- Number 4 (DISCIPLINE & ORGANISED): It relates to neat, tidy and good with details. On a broader level we can say an individual is practical and hardworking too. Also represents order and balance.
- Number 5 (BALANCE - Emotional & Mental): It is associated with balance. It relates to the balance and emotional stability of an individual. Also relates to freedom.
- Number 6 (HOME & FAMILY): It relates to creativity and love for home and family. It also relates to an individual being helpful with people and friendship. These individuals are very insecure for their home and family particularly for their children.
- Number 7 (DISAPPOINTMENTS): It relates to sacrifice. Their heart rules over their head. They learn through their losses or disappointments of four kinds which are Love, Emotional, Health, and Finance respectively.
- Number 8 (DISCIPLINE & ORGANISED): It is associated with discipline & organization. It relates to attention to detail.
- Number 9 (HUMANITARIAN): It is associated with humanitarianism. It relates to idealism, valour, and ambition.

The following is the table of the key words, a particular number comes in the grid how many times and what is said. If you have a repetitive number then it will have these effects -

Here are the numbers with their meaning in more detail-

Number 1

One time

- They cannot express their innermost thoughts.
- They can have difficulty understanding other people.

Two times

- They can communicate well.
- They are able to understand another person's opinion.

Three times

- They are like a chatterbox.
- However, they can also be silent and uncommunicative at times.

Four times

- They cannot express themselves yet very sensitive and compassionate.
- They sometimes create misunderstandings.
- It is difficult for them to relax.
- They are hyper most of the time.

Five times

- They are the least likely to be comfortable giving speeches to large audiences.
- However, they make excellent writers, artists or dancers.
- They have a tendency to overindulge in food, wine and lovers.

Number 2

One time

- They are sensitive and can easily have their feelings hurt.
- They are fast to recognize cunning people.

Two times

- They are very bright and intuitive, making them a good psychic.

Three times

- They are more sensitive and can be reclusive.

Four times

- They are at times so impatient and finicky that they can be very difficult to handle.
- They often prefer to be a loner as people find them a little weird.

Five times

- They are born complainers and cribbers.

Number 3

One time

- They have an excellent memory and a clear view of his goals.
- They are positive and natural born leaders.

Two times

- They are highly creative and are able to express their feelings very well.

Three times

- They are highly imaginative, living in their own world and it becomes at times difficult for them to relate with the outside world.
- They are compulsive day dreamers.

Four times

- They may appear to be paranoid due to their overactive imagination.

Number 4

One time

- They are very neat and tidy in their appearance and in their surroundings.
- They are involved in the systemic type of work.

Two times

- They are highly materialistic.
- They love to do their work and are very creative and artistic.

Three times

- They are athletic and hardworking, but mostly their energies are used in the wrong directions.

Four times

- They are good at work, especially involving their hands.
- They are laborious in their efforts and prefer doing jobs which require physical labour.

Number 5

One time

- They need lots of freedom in their relationships or at work. You cannot tie them down.
- They are very caring and well balanced and are constructive in their approach and good at motivating others.
- They make good leaders.

Two times

- They are determined and hard working.

Three times

- They are compulsive talkers who do not think before they speak.
- They generally repent what they say without thinking.
- They are daring and like to do off the beat things and love to travel to weird places.

Four times

- They get prone to accidents or also cause one itself. They become impulsive and do not think before they act.

Number 6

One time

- They are very close to their family and like to maintain pleasant surroundings.
- They are good advisers and listeners.
- People usually seek their advice.

Two times

- They are creative but also dominating parents who keep on worrying all the time without any serious reason.

Three times

- They are very temperamental.
- They are short tempered and need to control their foul tempers.
- Their creativity needs to be channelized which makes them great exponents in their chosen fields.

Four times

- They are a misfit as a child as they are highly creative and emotional.
- They like to throw tantrums but if given proper guidance in childhood they become geniuses in their chosen fields.

Number 7

One time

- They shall have a lesson by losing something close to him be it a person or object.

Two times

- They are interested in the spiritual world and life after death.

Three times

- They lead unfortunate lives surrounded by fraud, deceit and financial losses.
- But they are able to withstand all of it by their strong inner self.

Four times

- They have all the problems in this world pertaining to their health, home and finances.

Number 8

One time

- They are good with details and are conscientious. They have active minds and love to have varieties. They do not like doing routine jobs.

Two times

- They are very incisive and conscientious. They are more doers than listeners.
- Once they make decisions they stick to it.

Three times

- They are very materialistic and greedy.
- They make excellent businessmen and they want the very best for themselves.
- They have all the luxuries that money can buy.

Four times

- They are very restless and constantly in need of change.
- They either travel a lot or are usually behind the bars.

Number 9

One time

- They possess enough intelligence to choose between right and wrong.
- It represents learning on the mental level.

Two times

- They are intellectually inclined and also critical of others as they think they are the only ones with higher intelligence.

Three times

- They are someone who is a giving and idealistic person.
- They generally like to exaggerate a situation.

Four times

- They are super intelligent and at the same time they live in their own world or are labelled as loners.
- If their energies and intelligence are channelized properly they are capable of producing a positive result in our society and make wonderful leaders.

CHAPTER SIX

IMPACT OF MISSING NUMBERS

Numbers that are completely missing from the chart indicate lessons that the person has to learn this lifetime. Knowing what numbers our friends and families are missing in their charts allow us to know what they are struggling to learn. This enables us to be more understanding and supportive. Without this knowledge we might criticise others for their performance in certain areas, which never works. By knowing their missing numbers we can help them in their difficult areas and encourage them to lead a more successful life.

Everyone has at least one number missing from his or her chart.

Missing Numbers
1. 2. 3. 4 5. 6. 7. 8. 9.

Number 1

In this century we will find people without the number 1 in their charts. This has been impossible for a thousand years. People missing the number 1 will find it difficult to express their individuality, and will be more concerned with helping and nurturing others. They will be almost entirely without an ego. They will need to develop creative outlets of some sort, as this will allow them to express their emotions more constructively.

Number 2

People without number 2 in their charts are lacking sensitivity and intuition. Consequently, they will make many mistakes by ignoring the still, small, quiet voice within. They are inclined to be impatient and unpunctual. There is a tendency in these people to try to justify their actions, rather than admit they have made a mistake. These people need to learn to achieve balance in their lives.

Number 3

People without number 3 in their charts lack confidence and find it hard to express themselves. They are inclined to underestimate themselves and be overly self-effacing. They find it hard to think logically when faced with distractions. They need to learn to accept themselves as they are, then move forward gaining confidence and self-esteem at every step.

Number 4

People without number 4 find it difficult to work on a set routine. They are frequently disorganised and lacking in motivation. Consequently, they seldom achieve much until they have altered the way they look at life. They need to learn to be better organised and to work for what they want. Because the number 4 is the number of dexterity, people lacking it are seldom good with their hands. As they develop more patience and tolerance life becomes easier for them.

Number 5

People without number 5 find it difficult to get to goals; they lack drive and versatility. They need constant motivation from others. These people need to learn to set realistic goals and complete them before starting at others. A missing number 5 is very common.

Number 6

People without number 6 need to learn to give more to themselves. They tend to hide their innermost feelings from others. This usually relates to difficulties with one of their parents (often father) in early life. These people experience problems in their relationships until they learn to be more open and free.

Number 7

People without number 7 are inclined to be inconsiderate of other people's feelings. They are disorganised in their feelings. They are disorganised in their daily life. They have little or no interest in spiritual or metaphysical matters.

They find it hard to be self-sufficient and dislike being left on their own. They need to learn to express their inner feelings and become more relaxed around others.

Number 8

People without number 8 are poor at handling their financial matters. They can be overtly careless or too trusting and suffer financially as a result. They also lack motivation and leave tasks unfinished. They need to learn to control a natural impulsiveness and think before acting.

Number 9

It is impossible for any one born in the twentieth century to be missing this number, but many people born in the twenty-first century will not have it. People with missing number 9 tend to overlook the feelings and needs of others. They are detached and oblivious of what is going on in the lives of others. They need to learn to give to themselves, and become true humanitarians.

CHAPTER SEVEN

THE ARROWS OF STRENGTH AND WEAKNESS

There are fifteen arrows or lines that can appear in the chart. The arrows of strength occur when three numbers appear together in a row, horizontally, vertically, or diagonally. The arrows of weakness occur when three empty boxes appear together in a row, again horizontally, vertically, or diagonally.

These arrows are sometimes known as the Arrows of Pythagoras. It is possible that Pythagoras did use them, but if so, they were lost at least to the Western world until the 1930s when they were rediscovered by Dr. Hettie Templeton and published in her book 'Numbers and Their Influence'.

Arrows do not appear in every chart. Wolfgang Amadeus Mozart (born January 27, 1756) did not have any arrows in his chart. However, most charts do have them and when they appear they provide a valuable clue as to the person's makeup and personality. Some people have more than one arrow in their chart and, providing these are arrows of strength, they indicate significant capabilities and strength of character.

However, it is not always what we are given that counts. I have encountered many people with remarkable charts who have achieved little in life, and also met people with apparently difficult charts who have persevered and overcome their limitations. Later on, we will look at the chart of Indira Gandhi, who is an excellent example of someone with an extremely difficult chart who went on to make her mark on the world.

The Arrows of Strength

However, it is not always what we are given that counts. I have encountered many people with remarkable charts who have achieved little in life, and also met people with apparently difficult charts who have persevered and overcome their limitations. Later on, we will look at the chart of Indira Gandhi, who is an excellent example of someone with an extremely difficult chart who went on to make her mark on the world.

Having only 2 numbers in a row, column or diagonal indicates an above average ability in that characteristic. Having only 1 number indicates a below average ability.

Having no numbers in a row has an entirely different meaning - Negative Arrows.

Remember that having these abilities is not as important as what we do with them.

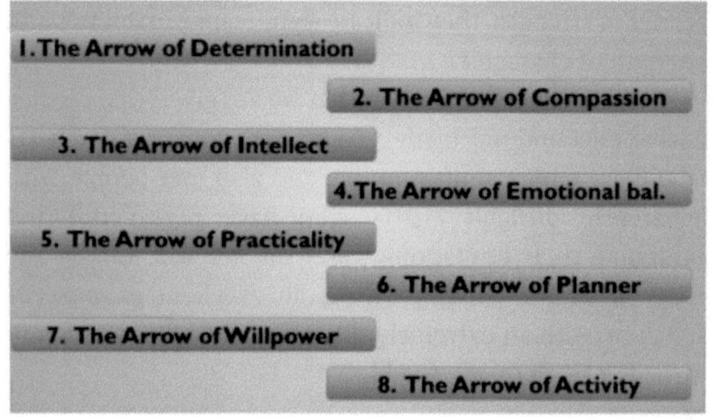

A. The Arrow of Determination

This arrow is made up of the numbers 1, 5 and 9. It is frequently found, as everyone born during the 1950s possesses it. As its name indicates, it makes people born with it determined and persistent. They are also enterprising, intense, and progressive. They are patient and prepared to wait for whatever it is they have set their minds on.

However, it is not always easy to be patient for long periods of time, and these people need to learn to control their temper. This is particularly the case if the number 4 is missing from their chart.

Margaret Thatcher (born October 13, 1925) is a good example of someone with an arrow of determination. She needed to develop patience and persistence in the long years before she achieved power.

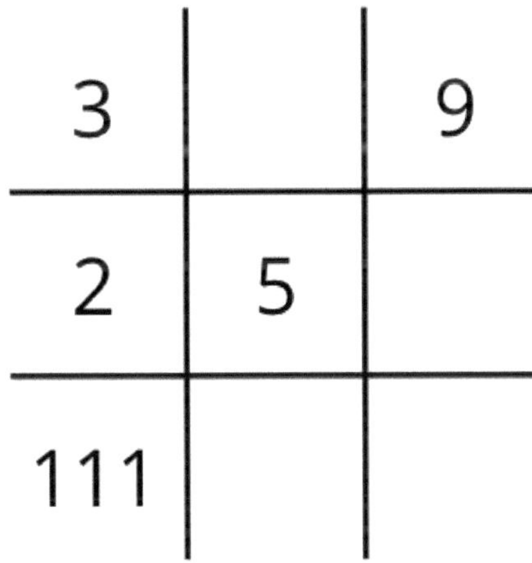

Lo Shu Chart of Margaret Thatcher

This arrow is found in the same position as in the West, and is made up of the numbers 8, 5 and 2. People with this arrow are patient, persistent, and determined. They are happy to bide their time until the moment is right, then act with decisiveness.

No matter what happens to them they never lose sight of thcir goals.

Someone born May 18, 1926, in the lunar calendar would have the arrow of determination.

	99	2
	55	
8	11	6

B. The Arrow of Compassion

This arrow is made up of the numbers 3, 5 and 7. People with this combination develop a strong faith and philosophy of life. This is normally caused by life's experiences; consequently these people often lead sad lives. However, as they mature, they develop an inner serenity and a strong faith that sustains and comforts them. Many people with this arrow have a strong interest in music.

This arrow is sometimes known as the arrow of mysticism. It is interesting to note that everyone born in the twentieth century with an arrow of compassion will also have the arrow of determination.

Elton John (born March 25, 1947) is a good example of someone with an arrow of compassion. His faith and philosophy come across vividly in much of his musical work.

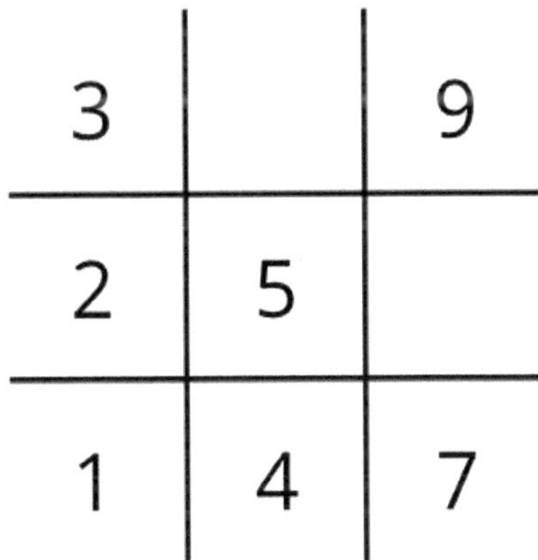

This arrow follows the path of the Arrow of Compassion in the Western chart, and consists of the numbers 4, 5 and 6. People with this arrow are compassionate, caring people who often make a career out of helping others. They are sensitive, often intuitive, and have an uncanny ability to understand other people's needs. These people can appear to be shy, particularly in the growing-up years. As children, they are well behaved, quiet, and gentle.

A person born April 15, 1966, in the lunar calendar would have the arrow of emotional balance.

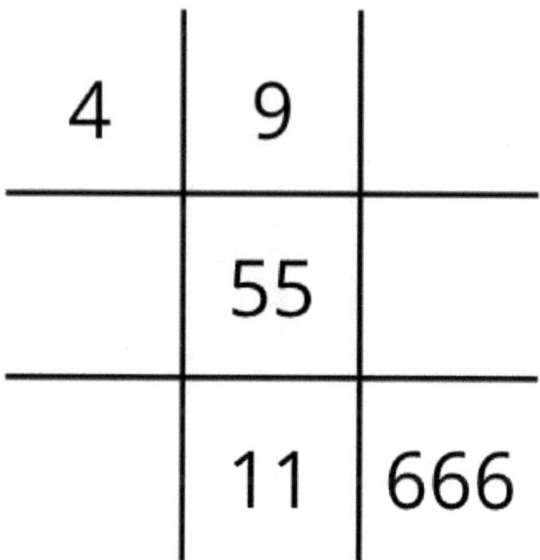

C. The Arrow of Intellect

The arrow of intellect is made up of the horizontal row of 3, 6 and 9. These are all the mental numbers and give those who possess them a good mind and excellent memory. These people are inclined to use their intellect at the expense of their emotions.

They may also tend to look down on people who are not their intellectual equals. Apart from this, they are well balanced and enjoy helping others. Home and family are important to them.

George Orwell (born June 25, 1903) is a good example of someone with an arrow of intellect. Orwell also had the arrows of determination and the planner in his chart, so he was gifted with enormous potential. His literary career took off when he published Down and Out in Paris and

London in 1933. Today he is best known for his satirical books, but he also wrote more general works and a series of essays on leading authors and their works.

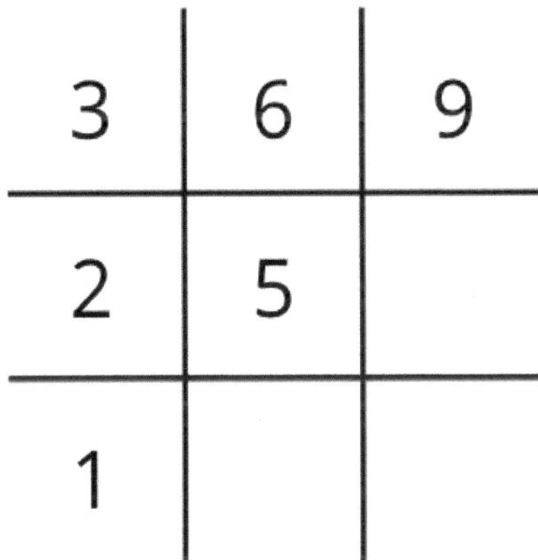

This arrow is in the same position as it is in the Western grid, but the numbers it comprises are 4, 9 and 2. The presence of these three numbers gives intellectual ability and an excellent memory.

This arrow belongs to people who are analytical, articulate, and logical, but who sometimes consider themselves to be superior to others.

Next century we will find a few people who do not have any numbers on the Spiritual or Material Planes. These people will be so overwhelmed by their thoughts that they run the risk of becoming mentally unbalanced. They will find it very hard to relax and unwind, and they will need constant support and help from others.

Someone born April 12, 1919, in the lunar calendar would have the arrow of intellect.

4	999	2
3		
	111	

D. The Arrow of Emotional Balance

The arrow of emotional balance is composed of the numbers 2, 5 and 8 in the Emotional Plane. People with this combination in their charts are understanding, compassionate and emotionally well balanced. They can easily understand and empathise with other people's point of view. They are also very natural healers.

This is an extremely strong arrow because of the presence of the 5. When people with this arrow decide to do something they don't stop halfway. They achieve their goals.

The celebrated actor Sean Connery (born August 25, 1930) is a good example of someone with an arrow of emotional balance in his chart.

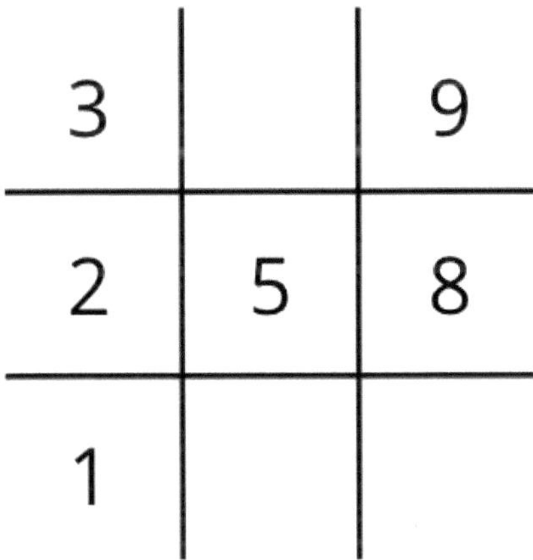

The Arrow of Spirituality - This arrow is particularly interesting as it is made up of the numbers 3, 5 and 7, the same numbers as in the Western version of this same arrow. However, instead of crossing the chart diagonally from the top left to the bottom right, it occupies the central, horizontal row.

The interpretation of this arrow is virtually identical to that used in the West. It emphasises the feelings, emotions, and spiritual aspects of the people who have it. It indicates a serious approach to life and an inner calm and serenity that seldom appears before middle age.

A person born March 17, 1953, in the lunar calendar would have the arrow of spirituality.

	9	2
33	5	7
8	11	

E. The Arrow of Practicality

The arrow of practicality is made up of the numbers 1, 4 and 7 on the Practical Plane. Not surprisingly, people with this arrow in their charts are capable with their hands. This may simply mean they work hard, but they can also express it as some form of creativity. These people are usually the "salt of the earth", being down to earth, capable, practical and easy to get along with.

This arrow usually relates to physical talents, but it can also be related to mental dexterity as well. These people are prepared to work long and hard for anything that they believe in.

Winston Churchill (born November 30, 1874) is a good example of a person with the arrow of practicality. Despite his privileged background and upbringing, he always had the "common touch" and related well with others. He also enjoyed working with his hands, constructing enormous brick walls and painting pictures.

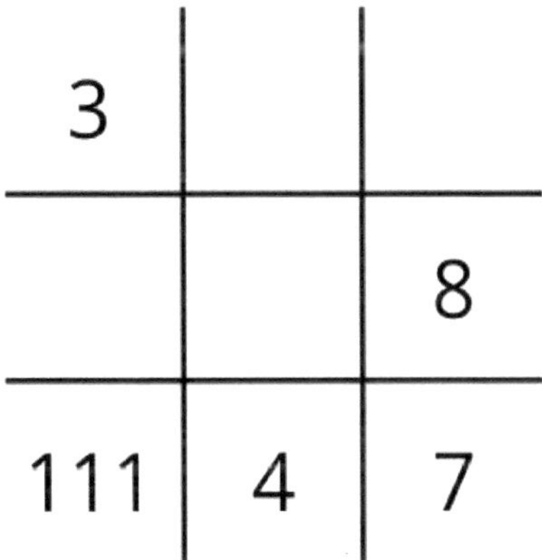

The Arrow of Prosperity - This arrow is in the bottom horizontal row, in the same position as the arrow of practicality on the Western chart. It is made up of the numbers 8, 1 and 6.

People with the arrow of prosperity excel in the business and commercial worlds. They are interested in money for its own sake, and are not usually interested in the higher values of life.

People who have the arrow of prosperity, but also have no numbers on the Spiritual Plane, are cold, calculating, and unfeeling. They achieve great material success, but do so by ignoring the feelings and needs of others.

A person born June 18, 1974, in the lunar calendar would have the arrow of prosperity.

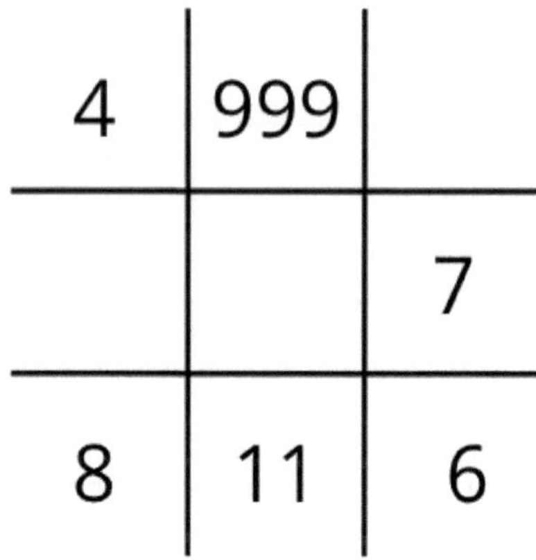

F. The Arrow of The Planner

The arrow of the planner consists of the first vertical column: numbers 1, 2 and 3. People with this combination have at least one number in each of the Mental, Emotional and Practical Planes. They are well-organized people who enjoy planning ahead and achieving their goals. Their weakness is in being undisciplined with the details. These people express themselves well and enjoy lengthy discussions on subjects that interest them.

They can also be studious and completely immerse themselves in their studies, becoming oblivious to everything around them.

Andrew Lloyd Webber, the famous British composer of musicals (born March 22, 1948), is a good example of someone with the arrow of the planner.

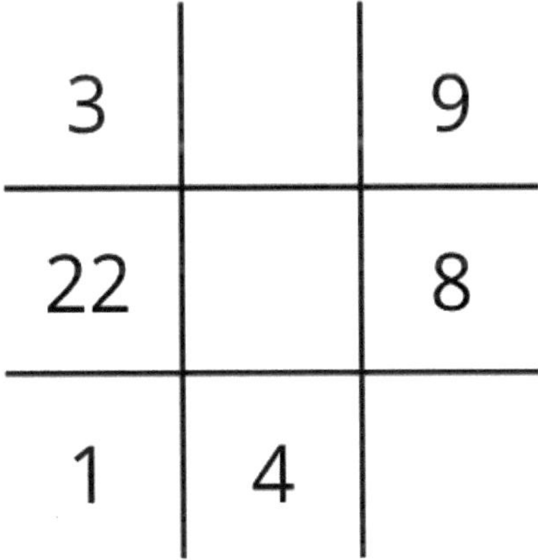

The Arrow of the Planner - This arrow is in the same position in both the solar and lunar charts. However, in the Eastern chart it consists of the numbers 8, 3 and 4. The basic meaning of this arrow is similar in both charts, but the Chinese idea of a planner is someone who is shrewd, cunning, and not very ethical. Consequently, it is sometimes known, fairly or not, as the "Politician's Arrow."

Someone born May 18, 1943, in the lunar calendar would have the arrow of the planner.

44	99	
3	5	
8	11	

G. The Arrow of Willpower

The arrow of willpower is a vertical column comprising the numbers 4, 5 and 6. It is an uncommon arrow, but one that gives considerable strength and endurance. People with this arrow in their charts are inclined to be self-centred, dynamic, and unbelievably persistent. They tend to be unaware of the feelings of others and can unwittingly hurt others in their drive to reach their own goals.

However, they make extremely good friends. Once someone with this arrow becomes your friend, nothing will break the friendship.

These people often experience major problems in their lives, but remain positive and optimistic. Invariably, they find resolutions.

Film star Gregory Peck (born April 5, 1916) is a good example of someone with the arrow of willpower.

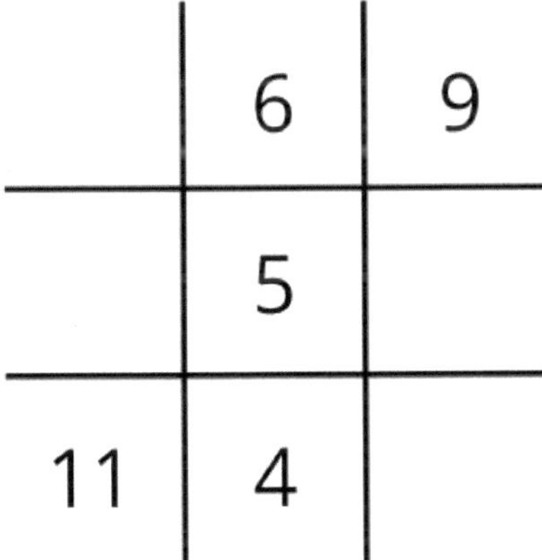

The Arrow of Willpower - This arrow is in the same position as it is in the Western grid, but contains the numbers 1, 5 and 9. (These numbers make up the arrow of determination in the Western version of the chart.) People with this arrow are stubborn. persistent, and determined. They are inclined to be argumentative and have strong opinions on a variety of subjects. This arrow is regarded as a symbol of success, because people with it steadily persist until they reach their ultimate goals.

Someone with a lunar birthday of September 15, 1955, would have the arrow of willpower.

	99	
	555	
8	11	6

H. The Arrow of Activity

The arrow of activity comprises the numbers 7, 8 and 9. People with this arrow in their charts need to express themselves through action. They need to be busy, either physically or mentally. They dislike confined spaces and prefer being outdoors with plenty of room around them. They have a tendency to be nervous and express themselves well with words on paper.

Richard Simmons (born July 12, 1948) is an interesting example of someone with the arrow of activity.

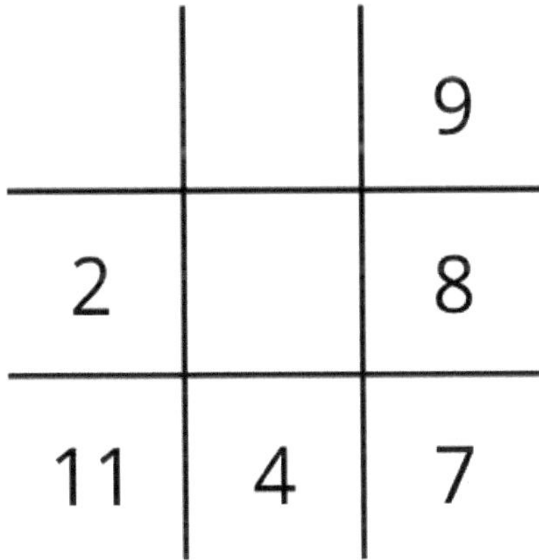

The Arrow of Action - This arrow occupies the same position as the arrow of activity in the Western chart. This is not surprising, as one of the keywords for this arrow is action. It consists of the numbers 6, 7 and 2. People with this arrow need to be busy, and love physical activities. They enjoy exercise and participating in sports. They have tremendous reserves of energy and are happiest when expanding it on some physical challenge.

A person born July 12, 1960, in the lunar calendar would have the arrow of action.

	99	2
3		7
	11	6

The Arrow of Weakness

There are 8 arrows of weakness depending on the row missing in the grid, after completing the numbers from your date of birth (as explained earlier).

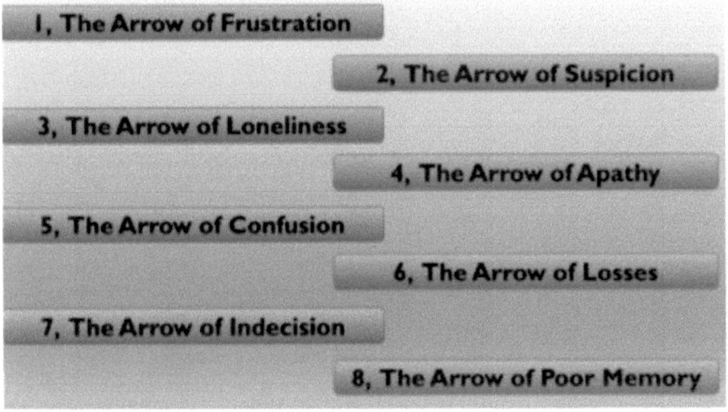

1, The Arrow of Frustration
2, The Arrow of Suspicion
3, The Arrow of Loneliness
4, The Arrow of Apathy
5, The Arrow of Confusion
6, The Arrow of Losses
7, The Arrow of Indecision
8, The Arrow of Poor Memory

The Arrows of Weakness

A. The Arrow of Frustration

The arrow of frustrations is a diagonal arrow created by the absence of the numbers 2, 5 and 8.

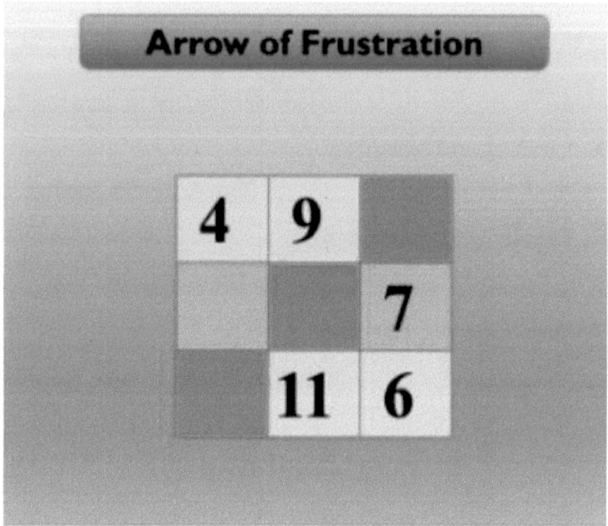

This arrow indicates many setbacks and frustrations. In the East it is regarded as a sign of consistent failure. People who have this arrow should try to learn from every experience and think carefully before acting. Someone born on June 19, 1974 in the lunar calendar would have the arrow of frustrations.

4	99	
		7
	11	6

B. The Arrow of Suspicion

This arrow is created by an absence of the numbers 4, 5 and 6.

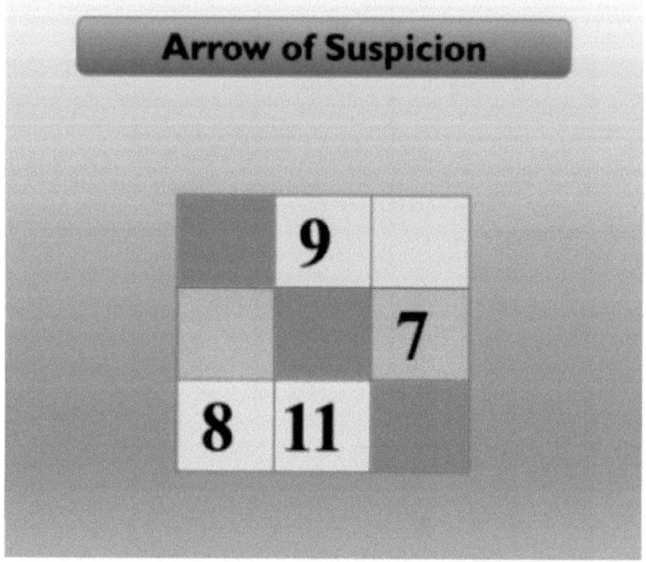

This arrow indicates people who are suspicious, cynical, and moody. They are inclined to worry and dwell on the negative side of life. This arrow revealed a "grey person" indicating someone who always lives in the shade and never comes out into the full light of day.

Someone born July 12, 1982 in the lunar calendar would have the arrow of suspicion.

	99	22
33		7
8	11	

C. The Arrow of Loneliness

This arrow consists of the absence of the numbers 3, 5 and 7 in the centre horizontal row.

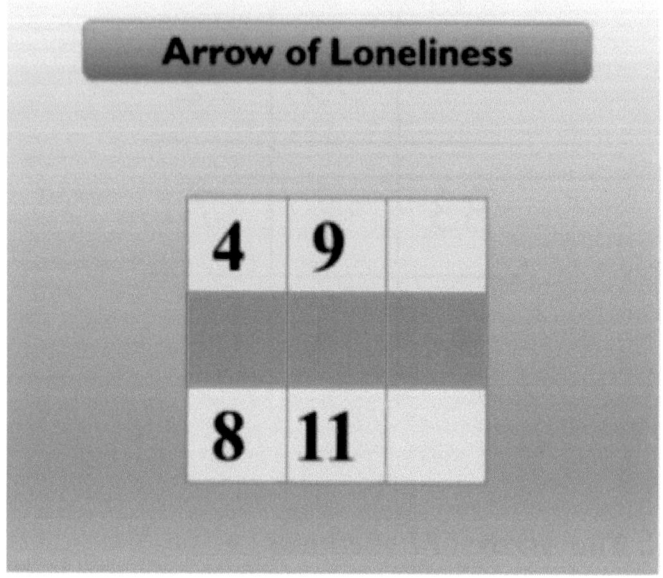

This arrow denotes a lack of feelings. People with this arrow are so intent on achieving their goals that they forget their friends and family, and consequently lack joy, love and laughter in their lives. They usually suffer enormously from loneliness in their old age.

Someone born August 28, 1986, in the lunar calendar would have the arrow of loneliness.

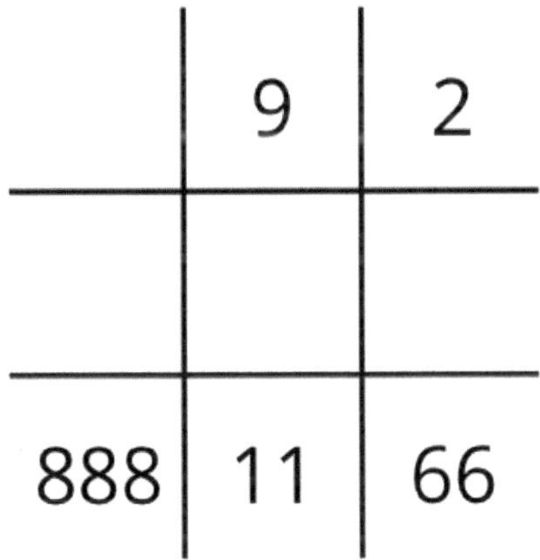

D. The Arrow of Apathy

This arrow is created when the chart lacks the numbers 2, 7 and 6 in the last vertical row.

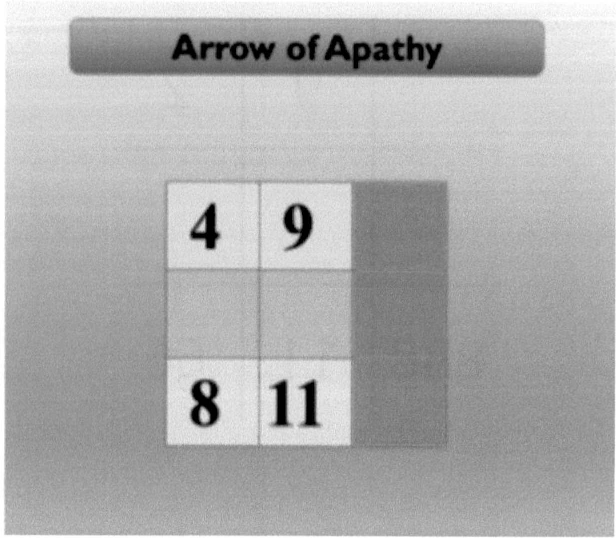

People with the arrow of apathy lack motivation and fail to grasp opportunities, even when freely handed to them. These people are indecisive, frightened of taking risks, and generally achieve only a fraction of what they could do if they applied themselves.

Someone born May 14, 1983, in the lunar calendar would have the arrow of apathy.

4	9	
3	55	
8	11	

E. The Arrow of Confusion

This arrow is caused by a lack of the numbers 4, 3 and 8 in the chart. It occupies the left-hand vertical column.

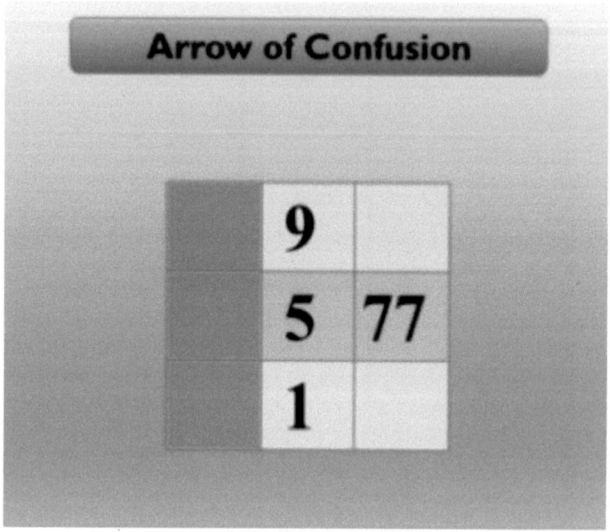

People with this arrow are not logical, methodical, or organised. They live from day to day, seldom making long-term plans. When they do, they usually sabotage the plans before they bear fruit.

Someone born July 5,1975, in the lunar calendar has the arrow of confusion.

	9	2
	55	77
	11	6

F. The Arrow of Losses

This arrow is created by an absence of the numbers 8, 1 and 6 in the bottom horizontal row.

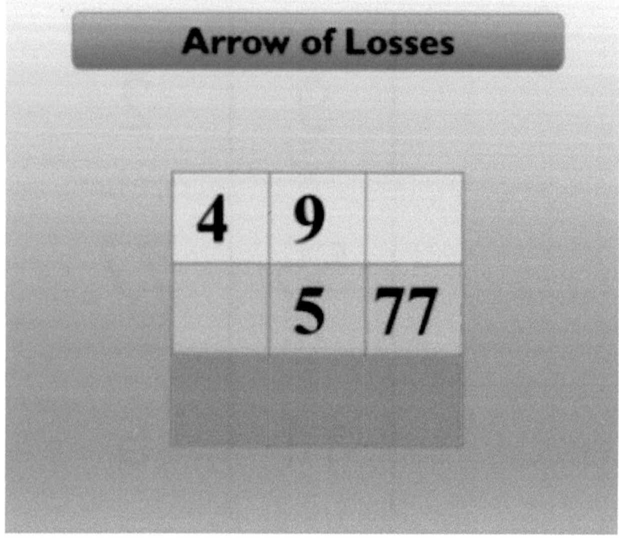

Consequently, nobody has had this arrow in their charts for the last thousand years, but it will appear again in the twenty-first century. These people will try to make money by participating in get-rich-quick schemes. They will constantly fail in these, and will not realise until middle age that if they had put the same amount of effort into a single, worthwhile goal they would have achieved success.

People born April 23, 2035, in the lunar calendar will have the arrow of losses.

4		22
33	55	

G. The Arrow of Indecision

This arrow is created by an absence of the number 9, 5 and 1 in the centre vertical row.

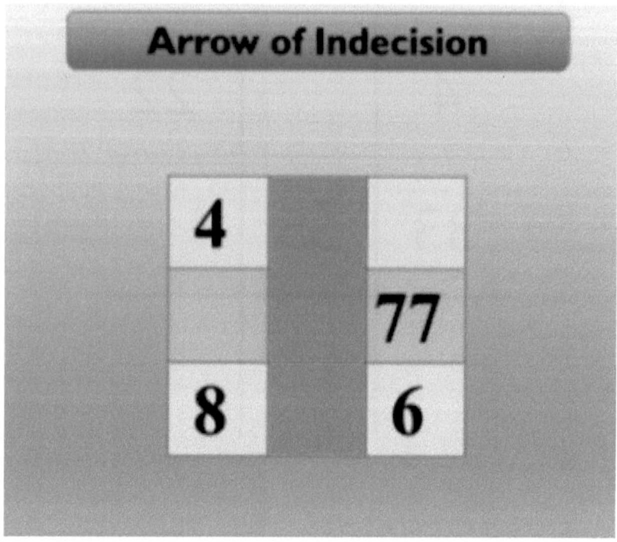

No one has had this arrow for the last one thousand years, but we will start to see it in the twenty-first century. People with this arrow have a desperate desire to be accepted and liked. Consequently, they can be easily led and swayed by others. They will find it extremely hard to stand up for what they believe in as they want to please everyone and are unable to express views that other people might not accept. Someone born on July 4th 2002 would have the above arrow.

4		22
		7
		6

H. The Arrow of Poor Memory

This arrow is created by an absence of the numbers 4, 9 and 2 in the top horizontal row.

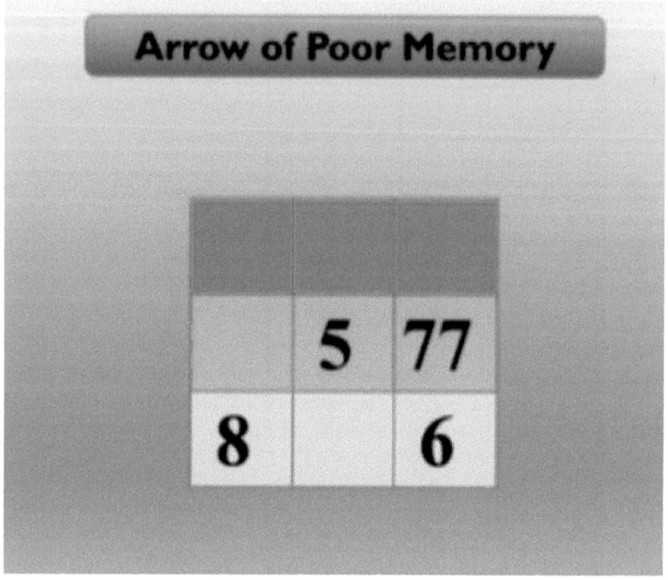

This arrow will not be found until the thirty-first century. Everyone born in the last century has had a 9 in his or her chart and everyone born in the next one thousand years will have a 2. People with this arrow start out in life with strong intellectual capabilities that gradually weaken as the person matures. These people are also frequently overwhelmed by the vivid nature of their thoughts and can suffer from mental imbalance. Someone born on May 3th 3087 would have this arrow of poor memory.

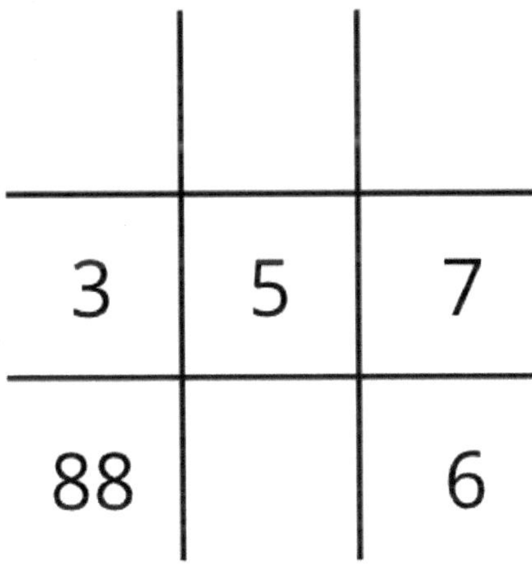

The Four Small Arrows

In the Far East, there are also four small arrows created by joining the four middle numbers of the outside horizontal and vertical rows. These are the small arrows joiningthenumbers1and3,3and9,9and7,and7and1.

A. The Arrow of Detail and Deceit

This is the arrow created when the chart contains both a 1 and a 3. People with this combination enjoy the details of things. In fact, if there is more than one of each number the person is inclined to be a perfectionist.

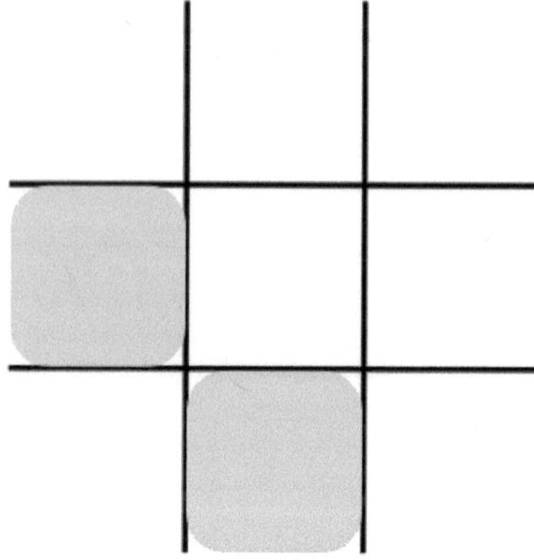

There is a negative side to this arrow. People with it are inclined to be dishonest when it suits them. They may lie about something or conceal the truth to protect themselves. In China this is sometimes known as the Criminal Line, but in my experience it belongs more to people who lie, rather than people who commit robberies or crimes of violence.

Someone born March 13, 1967, in the lunar calendar would have the arrow of detail and deceit.

B. The Arrow of Litigation

This arrow is created when the chart contains both the numbers 3 and 9. People with this combination are inclined to argue and become involved in disputes of all kinds. If these get too serious they have to be settled in a court of law, which is why this combination is known as the arrow of litigation.

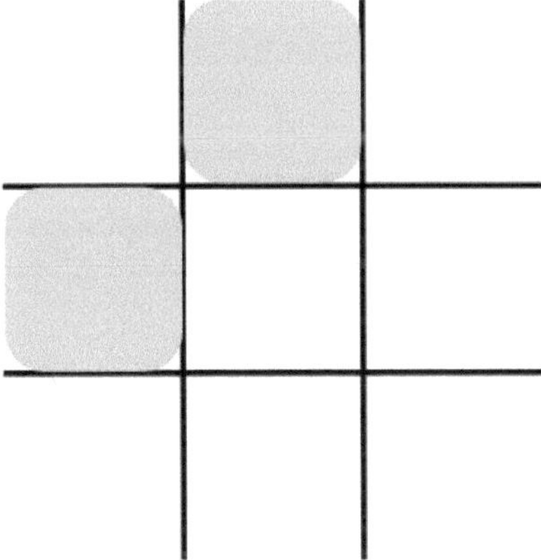

Someone born July 3, 1985, in the lunar calendar would have the arrow of litigation.

C. The Arrow of Peace of Mind

This arrow is created when the chart contains both the numbers 3 and 9. People with this combination are inclined to argue and become involved in disputes of all kinds. If these get too serious they have to be settled in a court of law, which is why this combination is known as the arrow of litigation.

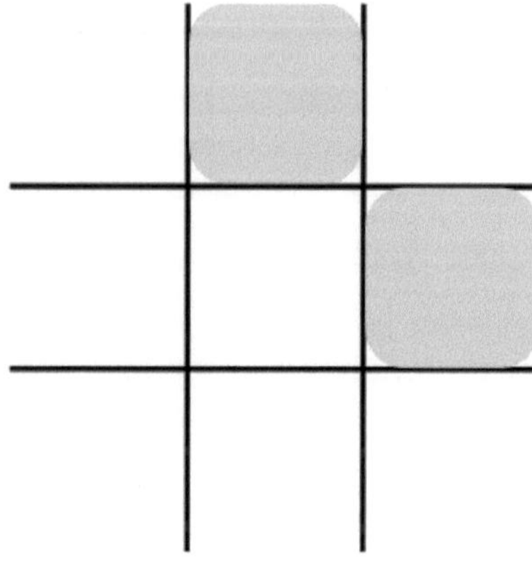

Someone born July 8, 1966, in the lunar calendar would have the arrow of peace of mind.

D. Arrow of Science

People with charts that contain the numbers 1 and 7 are interested in the mysteries of the world we live in.
They enjoy searching for the hidden truths and can become so involved with their studies that they get lost in research.

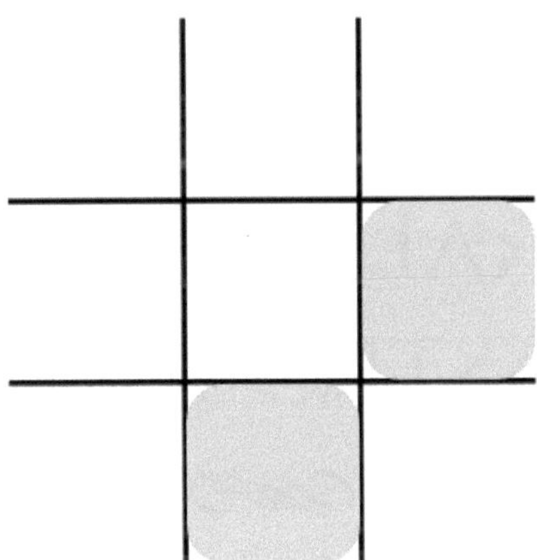

They are usually interested in the sciences (frequently those that concern the oceans), which is how this arrow got its name.

Someone born May 27, 1974, in the lunar calendar would have the arrow of science.

CHAPTER EIGHT

PARALLELS WITH ASTROLOGY

There are 9 planets in astrology and each and every planet corresponds to the 9 numbers we have in Lo Shu numerology. The characteristics of each planet is seen in the numbers and their placement (presence) in the chart.

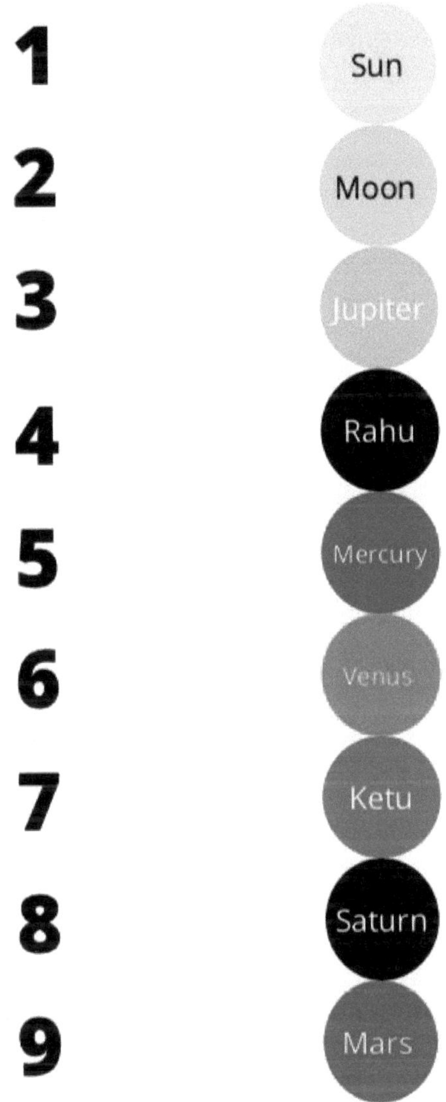

Loshu Numbers and their corresponding Planets

Each planet has its specific traits. Let us understand one by one.

Sun:

Sun is the Atma (soul) of all planets and the person as well. It possesses various positive traits such as being a fatherly figure, having immense strength, holding self- respect and authority. It is Sun to show how a person projects himself onto the world. If a strong Sun represents energy and authority, a weak Sun can make a person ego-centric/ overconfident. You may need a strong Sun when it comes to your career and profession, but not when you deal with personal relationships.

Mars:

Mars denotes courage, passion, bravery, strength and confidence. But in many aspects of life, you don't need all this equally. A strong Mars can help you in your career and profession but can adversely affect your married life.

Moon:

Moon represents the mind, acts as the mother of all, imparts love, peace of mind, positivity, and emotions. A strong Moon helps a person in all stages of life, but a weak Moon can bring troubles like a flickering mind or even depression.

Venus:

Venus represents love, relationship, romance, beauty, sex life, relationships, be it with the spouse/business associates. Many may not know, but a good Venus is an essence for your professional life. So at what stage you need support from Venus is to be decided by you.

Mercury:

Mercury represents speech, Intelligence, grasping power, alertness, and logic. Though Mercury plays a significant role throughout life, it assumes more importance during the early stage of education.

Jupiter:

represents knowledge. It helps a person more when it reaches the stage of education and career, so may not have that significance in the early age of the person or, say, initial childhood.

Rahu:

Rahu brings name and fame, but spoiled Rahu brings humiliation. Rahu is the planet for worldly desires, manipulation apart from many other significations attached to him. The heavy impact of Rahu in the initial age of life can make a person too much involved in mobile phones/ internet-related activities and the result we know.

Rahu is a shadowy and mysterious plant which, if it acts negatively, tends to make a person over-ambitious, over-confident, and "I don't care" type of attitude. It makes a person know no limit or cross all limits and the result we know when we hear about Top Babas, Businessmen,

Bureaucrats and Politicians in the worst phase of their life. So how you make use of it depends on you. You stay under control, Rahu will play a good role, you brag or over-step, Rahu will devastate. So the results of Rahu are in your hands.

Ketu:

Ketu shows spirituality but detachment also. This is again a shadowy planet of no physical existence. Ketu is known to be malefic to worldly desires and spiritually benefic. So an adverse effect of Ketu can turn a person away from mundane and worldly desires, including Love and romance, at the age when you need them most.

Saturn:

Saturn is the Karmic planet that practically holds a person's life throughout with the type of Karmas one does. You step out, become extra ambitious, or commit wrong deeds; Saturn will punish you. Saturn plays the dual role of a teacher and a cop. It depends on what you want Saturn to do to you. Saturn delays things in your life. Everything comes with hardship and time. Nothing comes easy with saturn in action. It brings consistent failure, constant frustrations in any line of work. In other way saturn teaches you hard lessons of life.

CHAPTER NINE

MARRIAGE & LOVE LIFE

Find your Age of Marriage

As you already know How to get the driver and conductor number through the date of birth.
To find out the age of marriage we have to find out the king and queen number using the above two numbers.

King number is the addition of driver number with 9 twice i.e
King Number = Driver number + 9 + 9
Similarly,
Queen number = Conductor number + 9 + 9

Both these numbers provide the range of age where the possibility of marriage exists.
For example if the date of birth is 13 Jan 1989. The Driver number comes out to be 4 and the conductor number is 5. So,

- King number=4+9+9=22 = 4
- Queen Number=5+9+9=23 = 5

So the conclusion can be derived from it is that the marriage of this person will take place between 22-23 year of his/her age. If for some reason the person decides to delay it because of the career or other reasons. Then in that case the next possible phase of marriage will arrive after the next cycle of 9 years. We will further add 9 to the formula to come to that age.

Another method of knowing if the person is going to have an early marriage or late marriage is through the Lo Shu Chart.

If in the chart diagonal number sequence 4,5,6 or 2,5,8 is present, then this is the case of early marriage before the age of 27 otherwise the marriage can take place even after 30-35 depending upon the other absent numbers.

For Love marriage or finding your own partner a person has to have the numbers 4 and 7 in their charts. 4 and 7 represent Rahu and Ketu respectively. 4 makes one financially strong to take the responsibility in a relationship and 7 makes one self sufficient and self made, Number 7 does not need any approval they make up their mind and act. Otherwise the number 9 is important because number 9 shows the support of parents. In this case that support will be in the decision of marriage.

Other numbers like 1 and 2 also play their role here. Number 1 which is sun is for career and personality without that the confidence is missing in the person. Number 2 (Moon) is for happiness satisfaction contentment in life which is important for relation to sustain.

CHAPTER TEN

Marriage Problem/ Divorce

There are certain combinations which create the possibilities where there can be problems in the married life of a person. In certain cases these problems can even lead to divorce.

For this driver number of any date of birth is to be considered. As you already know by now that driver number is the addition of only birth date digits.
For example if the date of birth is 25 july 1990. The driver number is 2+5= 7.

Now there are certain combinations which should not happen in between the couple/partners.

If the driver number of both the partners are 3 & 6 or 8 & 9, then the problem is bound to happen. This combination is not allowed for a successful marriage. 3,6 or 8,9 can not go together, but the combination of 3 with 6 and 8 with 9 is considered fine.

Similarly, a similar number like 4 with 4 or 2 with 2 is also not a recommended combination. This is because number 4 makes a person very stubborn, when both the partners in a relationship are stubborn then it is very difficult to carry on.

Same happens with the number 2 combination. Number 2 makes a person emotional, if both partners are very emotional, both are not able to pick themselves up. Both rise and fall together, so this combination is also not good.

In Lo Shu grid, repetition of numbers like 9, 3, 8, 6 twice or thrice also creates a chart where problems can be seen in going along with others, not just in relationships but otherwise as well.

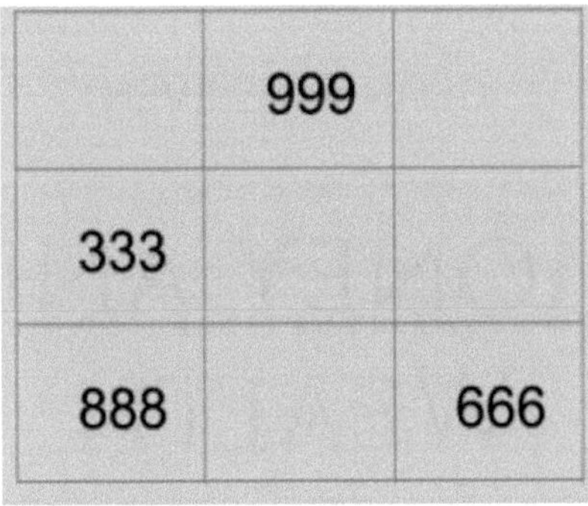

	999	
333		
888		666

In the combination above if a person is having any of these numbers repeated multiple times. Then the problem in marriage is bound to happen irrespective of what is there in the oher partners Grid. If the combination of one partner is good then the problem reduces somewhat.

If any of the combinations occur in the chart of the couples which we have discussed so far, then there is a high possibility of problems or in worst case it could even lead to divorce.

CHAPTER ELEVEN

MONEY AND WEALTH

Money or wealth generated depends on two diagonal lines. Some numbers in the Lo Shu grid are indicators of wealth. Some numbers are directly related to money, and some indicate the happiness and prosperity derived out of it. So overall all these numbers are important for understanding wealth and happiness.

Each Number in 'Lo Shu Grid' has their significance. 2 = Overall happiness.

- 4 = Wealth and prosperity.
- 5 = Well-being and stability.
- 6 = Spirituality, Presence of helpful people, foreign travel.
- 7 = Self Earning without any support
- 8 = Education, hard work, information and knowledge

Primary Wealth Indicator

4, 5, 6 forming a diagonal sequence if present in any chart, then it shows potential of huge earning by that individual. Number 5 is for stability in life. Number 4 is the money one earns during their lifetime. If 4 is repeated twice or several times that means the person is going to earn twice or thrice as much as his father has made money in their lifetime. Number 6 is the support one gets from friends, peers. Since we are talking about finance here this support can be related to finance here. With number 6 present one will not find it difficult to arrange loans from banks or other sources. Number 6 is Venus, so it also represents luxury, easy life.

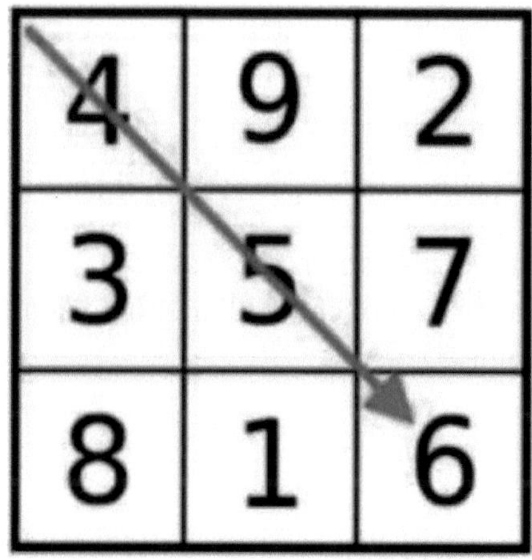

Secondary Wealth Indicator

2, 5, 8 forming a diagonal sequence in the grid is the secondary wealth indicator because it is less powerful than Primary Wealth Yoga. 2 here indicates the happiness and satisfaction in life. As it also represents the moon which is our mind. Good mind is important to lead a fulfilling life. Number 5 gives stability and number 8 gives knowledge, wisdom and capacity to work hard to achieve something.

If this arrow is present in any chart, then the person owns many properties at several places. He / She may have a career in real estate business also. Now the question can be why is it so? This is because the Numbers 2, 5, 8 represent the earth element and the matters related to land property buildings are related to earth only.

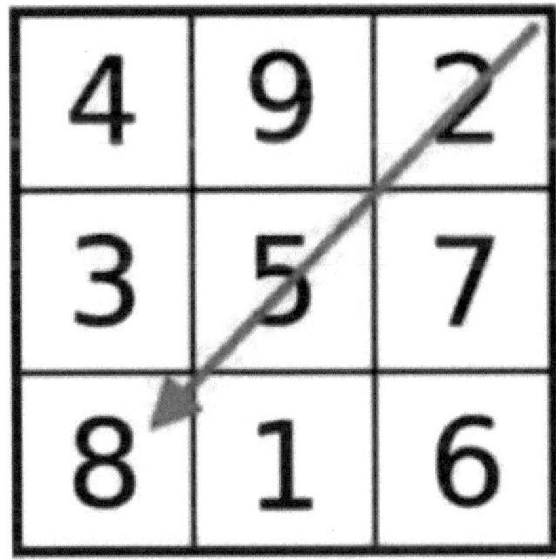

There is one more number outside the ambit of these two diagonal wealth arrows which is Number 7. One can own money through their own endeavour, or it can come from ancestral property, father or mother or other supports. Number 7 is the indicator of wealth earned through their own efforts.

Let us suppose that a person is having 4 & 7 in their chart, that means he / she will earn lots of money through their own efforts. If they are running any business, they will be actively involved in that. These are not Passive income or income from investment. These are direct active income through direct active participation.

How Much Money Will You Earn This Year?

To predict whether you will earn a lot of money in a particular year or not, you need to write down the year first.

Let us take one example here.

Date of Birth (DD/MM/YYYY) – 24/05/1990
Desired Prediction Year – 2016
So, in this case, in the original date of birth you will replace 'year of birth' by 'desired prediction year' i.e., 1990 to be replaced by 2016.
Now we have got some numbers from the above example.

They are:
24/05/2016=2,4,0,5,2,0,1,6
Next, we must calculate two important numbers, they are:

- Active Number (Driver number) = 2+4 (Birth Date) = 6
- Passive Number (Conductor number) (With changed year number of present year) = 2+4+5+2+1+6 (Birth DD/ Birth MM/ Desired YYYY) = 20 =2

For a person, the Active number will always remain the same, but the Passive Number will keep changing as per the desired year.

Now place these numbers in respective boxes as shown in the picture

4 Wealth & Prosperity		222
	5 Well Being	7
	1	66 Helpful People

See in above chart 4, 5 and 6 is forming a diagonal line without any number gap. This is called diagonal Primary Wealth Indicator Group. If such a diagonal number group is present, then that year the person will/ has earned a lot of money. This diagonal group is also called Primary Wealth Yoga Indicator in 'Lo Shu Grid'. There is also a Secondary Wealth Yoga Indicator in 'Lo Shu Grid' which will be a diagonal group of number 2, 5, 8.

If any number is missing to form the wealth indication (Primary or Secondary Wealth Yoga Indicator) then the person will face problem that number related part of life.

They are as following:

- 2 = Emotional imbalance or turmoil and wrong decisions.
- 4 = Lack of opportunity, money flow got stuck, unable to recover money, sometimes even debt.
- 5 = Lack of stability due to sudden major change in life
- 6 = Hidden and open enemies
- 8 = Wrong investment based on wrong information.

CHAPTER TWELVE

Case Study

Bill Gates

Born on 28 oct 1955

Bill Gates is an American business magnate, software developer, investor, author, and philanthropist. He is a co-founder of Microsoft. Bill Gates promotes the welfare of others through philanthropy and technology, which gives people a sense of hope in the world and therefore, makes him a hero. Bill Gates is inspiration to many because of his philanthropy work. He helps so many through his charitable donations.

What makes him do all this? Let us understand that –

Bill gates Date of Birth is 28 oct 1955. His Lo Shu grid looks like in the figure below.

4	9	2
	55	
8	111	

Loshu Chart of Bill Gates

As you can see in the above figure, the Plane of thought which includes 4,9,2 is complete, which makes him sharp intellectually and all the business decisions he makes are through his own intellect. He excelled in the technology field also having a plane of thought and number 5 (mercury) in his chart made him good in the technical field.

Presence of a secondary wealth arrow allowed him to have multiple investments. Had he not been a Microsoft owner he would definitely have succeeded as a real estate businessman also.

Will Plane of 9,5,1 is very strong with two 5 and three 1's makes him very tough mentally to persevere under critical circumstances.

Overall, the birth chart is such that in one way or another he would have done well in other fields also. In today's time the World business leaders do indulge in multiple sectors through their investments or other means. They do not rely on a single business. That is why they have become so big.

Jeff Bezos

Born on 12 Jan 1964

Jeffrey Preston Bezos (DOB- 12 Jan 1964) is an American entrepreneur, media proprietor, investor, and computer engineer. He is the founder and executive chairman of Amazon, where he previously served as the president and CEO. He is one of the richest men in the world at present.

What makes him rich and what does his LO Shu look like? We will see

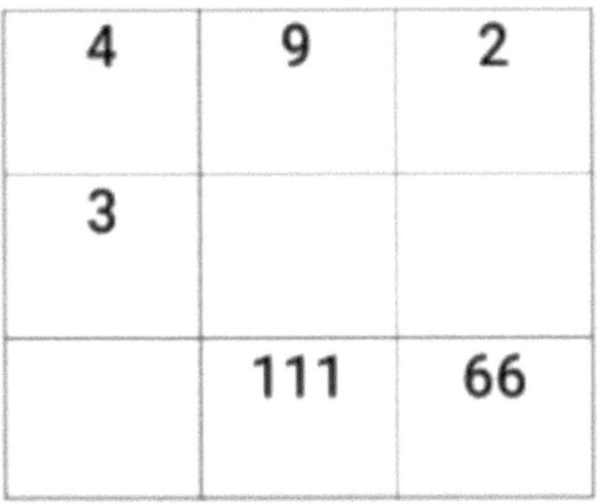

4	9	2
3		
	111	66

Loshu Chart of Jeff Bezos

Here you can see the number 5 is missing so the number which represents the stability in the life of a person is missing. But Mental Plane (4,9,2), Thought plane numbers (4,3) & Practical Plane number (1,6) are present making him an exceptional entrepreneur.

As we discussed earlier, 4,3 are wood elements indicating success in career. It also gives great vision and purpose towards the goal of life.

Repetition of number 1 multiple times shows one's fame and career. Both Bill Gates and Jeff Bezos have 111. making them well known around the world.

His missing number 8 must be getting compensated from anywhere in his life. Because inspite of missing number 8 in the Practicality plane (8,1,6). Presence of numbers 1 & 6 makes him very hard working and practical, his decision making comes from his own hard experiences of life even though he has a good thought plane (good mind, intelligence).

CHAPTER THIRTEEN

Remedies For Wealth and Money Problem

We need to take the help of Vastu, Feng Shui and Astrology related remedies here.
First let's discuss about Astrological remedies:
Every number of 'Lo Shu Grid' represents a planet in astrology. Following are the list of respective planets and their remedies according to astrology:

- 2 = Moon = Pearl
- 4 = Rahu = Gomed (Hessonite)
- 5 = Mercury = Emerald
- 6 = Venus = Diamond, White Zircon
- 8 = Saturn = Blue Sapphire, Amethyst

Remedies according to Vaastu and Feng Shui:

Number 2 in 'Lo Shu Grid' = Represents Southwest direction, Element is: Earth, and the Colour is: Yellow.
If number 2 is missing while creating Secondary Wealth Yoga then do the following:

If it is your relationship which is making your mind unstable, and you are unable to concentrate on financial improvement then place both of your (your partner and you) picture in a yellow, golden or black frame here.

If it is due to incapability of taking the right decision at the right time thus creating hindrances to develop or show your skill, then place a 'Brass Eagle' here.

Number 4 in 'Lo Shu Grid' = Represents Southeast direction, Element is: Wood, and colours are: Dark Green, Brown.
If number 4 is missing while creating Primary Wealth Yoga then place 4 'Long Bamboo Sticks' in a White / Brown

Flower Vase in this direction.

Number 5 in 'Lo Shu Grid' = Represents Centre position of the home, Element is: Earth. Colours: Yellow

If number 5 is missing while creating Primary and Secondary Wealth Yoga then hang crystal balls in this direction, preferably white or yellow.

Number 6 in 'Lo Shu Grid' = Represents Northwest direction, Element is: Metal. Colours: Grey.

If number 6 is missing while creating Primary Wealth Yoga then place a 'Pair Of Metal Elephants' in this direction.

Number 8 in 'Lo Shu Grid' = Represents Northeast direction, Element: very small amount of Earth. Colours: very light yellow.

If number 8 is missing while creating Secondary Wealth Yoga then place an OM symbol here in golden frame.

CHAPTER FOURTEEN

BUSINESS OR JOB

Some people do well in their jobs and some people start their own business and change their fortunes. What makes this distinction we will understand through Lo shu. In this chapter one will understand what is more beneficial for them to opt- Business or Job?

If in any chart action plane (2,7,6) is present along with the practical plane then doing some business is more beneficial.

Even if action plane (2,7,6) is with the mental plane (4,9,2), then also there is a good possibility of him/her being in some business. Other than these possibilities one having a job and being under some organisational structure is better for an individual.

4	9	2
		7
		6

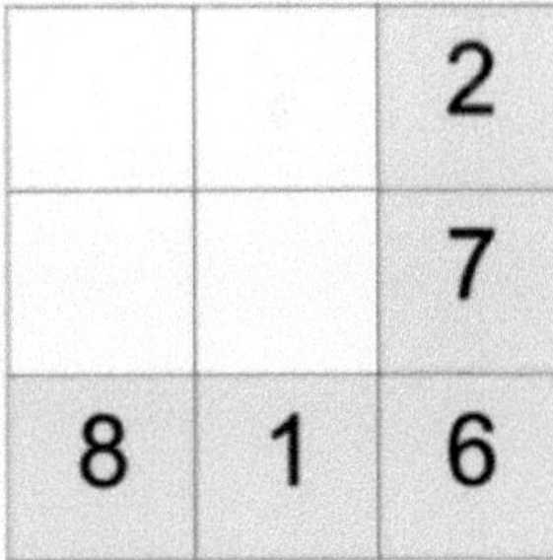

		2
		7
8	1	6

Doing business or a job is another thing and having success in what you are doing is another. So what guarantees success in Business or Job? The answer is number 4,3 and 5. If these numbers are present alongside the numbers present in action/mental or practical planes, then success comes easy with efforts put in.

Number 4 makes one a visionary. Number 3 gives the person a sense of purpose. The individual knows what he is doing and how he is going to do it. Number 5 gives the balance and stability in the environment to make things achievable. Number 4 and 3 are also the wood element which signifies success.

If the plane of practicality is present in any chart that means the person will achieve success through his/her hard work and good sense of decision making. On the other hand if the mental plane (4,9,2) is present, that means his/her success is through his own good intellect and mind.

Decisions made in 8,1,6 plane come through hard earned knowledge and through own experiences whereas decisions made in the mental plane are done through sharp intelligence and cleverness.

Action plane allows one to act despite all odds when other things support the actions taken gives the best results.

CHAPTER FIFTEEN

Stock Market Success

The Stock Market is one place where fortunes are made and broken every day. Some people make money everyday through trading, others invest for longer periods for bigger returns. One thing remains common among all is that everybody is here for some profit, nobody wants to lose this game. Lo shu chart is not only used in daily life choices but it's also used in making business decisions and the stock market is no exception.

It can also be used to see the potential success in the area of Stock trading. Trading is done based on the numbers in the stock market listing. There are certain numbers if present in the lo shu chart of an individual brings the chances of great success in this area. Numbers 4, 3, 8 and 5 are some important numbers which, if present in the chart, can really turn the fortunes of a person in the stock market. There are certain numbers which do favour the stock market trading according to Lo Shu.

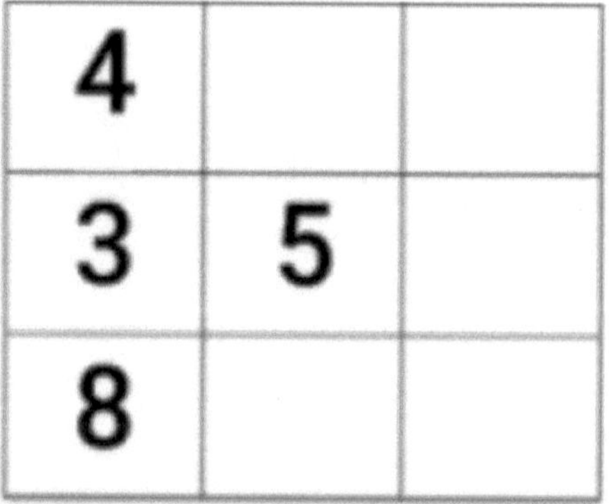

4		
3	5	
8		

Number 4,3,8 along with 5 favours stock trading. Number 5 is for mercury makes the individual good with numbers, statistics, and trade. Number 8 gives the knowledge through experience and information available. Number 3 gives a person acumen to see the upside and downside of things helps in planning intricately.

Number 4 shows the result of all which is money one earns through these efforts. Presence of numbers 4, 3, 8 also creates the Plane of Planning which makes one excellent planner and visionary. So, these numbers, if available in the Lo Shu chart, helps a person to excel in this field. Even if a person is having any two numbers out of these four numbers available let's say 4,8 or 3,5. Then that is good enough to try their luck in the Stock market.

Now we will understand with some case study how the Lo Shu chart of some of the famous personalities who have made fortunes through the stock market looks like.

Case Study

Warren Buffet

Born on 30 Aug 1930

Warren Edward Buffett is a well-known American business magnate, investor, and philanthropist. He is currently the chairman and CEO of Berkshire Hathaway. He has been the market player for several decades and made fortunes out of it. From his date of birth the Lo shu Chart looks like this-

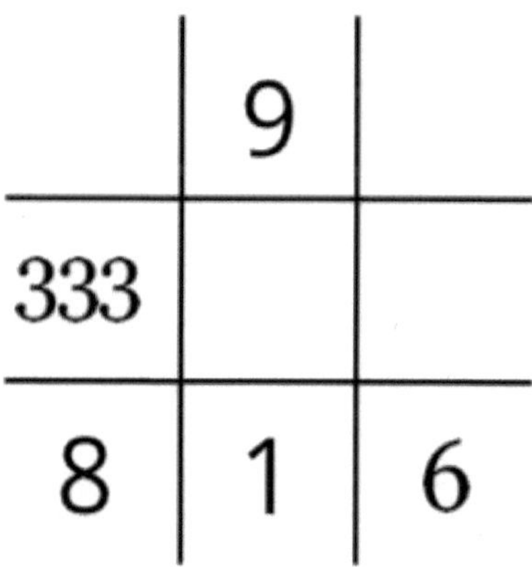

On the first look the chart looks very ordinary, but there is the practical plane 8,1,6 making it strong along with the presence of double 3. Out of the 4 numbers required the chart has the two numbers with the repeat of 3. The number 8 gives him the knowledge and experience in the field.

Practical plane makes him trust his own decisions which come from his own experiences. And the 33 makes the strong case here for him to be good at what he does. He is good at speculating and catching opportunities before others. Despite not having 5 in the middle and having absence of number 4, he has made himself an icon in this sector. This is one of those exceptional charts where the person exceeds what's provided to them by nature.

Bill H Gross

Born on 13 Apr 1944

William Hunt Gross is an American investor and fund manager, best known for co-founding Pacific. He made huge wealth in 40 years of his career through the stock market. This can be seen in his chart as well.

4444	9	
3		
8	11	

Repeating the number 4 times shows the huge wealth he made in his lifetime. Presence of 3 and 5 are also there, favouring his career success.

Note that Number 4 shows wealth and money but when it is multiple times, it can be said that he/she has made wealth more than those many times to what his father or ancestors have earned in their lifetime.

CHAPTER SIXTEEN

SUCCESS IN GLAMOUR INDUSTRY

Possibility of success in the glamour world or even in the world of Sport can be seen through the Plane of Action.

Since these people are the centre of attraction and action. Plane which represent them are Plane of Action which are 2,7 and 6.

Number 6 is for venus which gives luxury in life and support all around. Number 7 is the ability to achieve something through his/her own efforts, self made people have 7 in their charts.Number 2 gives the emotional well being, satisfaction, love and happiness in life.

Other numbers do play their role as well. Like number 1 gives good career fame, 9 gives energy and fight spirit which is important for sportsmen, 4,3 gives wealth and success.

Number 5 gives good communication and stability in all aspects of life.

Some people find it hard to break through so they take time to blossom and come into light through their hard work. These people have 8 playing that role in their success.

There are chance people do not have the complete action plane still they make it very big in their lives. How does that happen ? This happens because other numbers compensate for it.

Case Study

Leonardo DiCaprio

Born on 11 Nov 1974

Let us take an example of Leonardo DiCaprio. His date of birth is 11 Nov 1974

His Lo Shu Chart have a complete mental plane with 111 and double 7 (77)

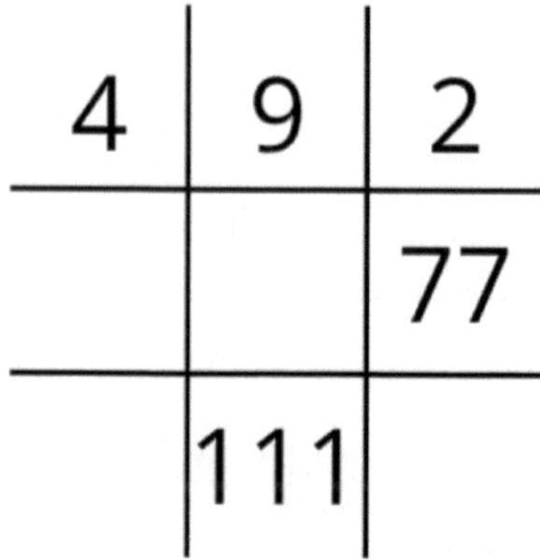

1 repeated three times gives him fame and success making him a global star.

7 repeating twice makes his ketu very strong. What he has achieved he has achieved on his own. 4 being present gives him success, wealth and prosperity and compensates for the missing of number 6 (venus). All the 5 elements earth, fire, water, metal and wood elements being present in the chart makes this very balanced chart.

Usain Bolt

Born on 21 Sept 1986

Take one more Example of Usain Bolt, He is the Global superstar and considered fastest man on the Planet. His Date of Birth is 21 Sept 1986

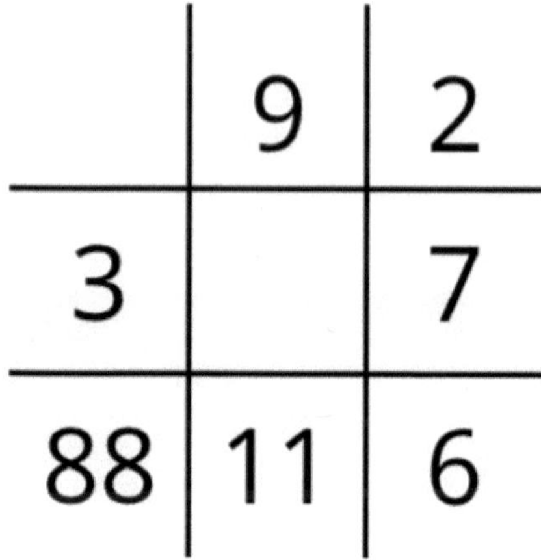

Action plane is complete in this chart along with the practical plane. He has achieved success through hard work. Number 8 twice in the practical plane shows this. He has a balanced chart even with missing 5 in this chart because all the 4 directions (East, West, North, South) are complete with the numbers making a proper balance.

CHAPTER SEVENTEEN

REMEDIES IN LO SHU

How to use Lo shu?

Let's take an example to understand how we can use the Lo Shu Grid to understand our life.

How to apply Lo-Shu Grid. Let's take one example of birth date 12 July, 1977 :-

Place the number of date of birth in the Lo-Shu square as shown:-

SE	SOUTH	SW
EAST		WEST

East				West
		9	2	
			777	
		11		

NE	NORTH	NW

Now we can observe that

(A) In the chart 3 & 4 (represent wood element) is missing thereby growth is missing in his life. **cure**: Green light in the East & South-East in bed room for enhancing growth.

(B) Number 5 & 8 (represent Earth element) is missing thereby whatever he speaks or acts will not be forceful thereby he is not properly rewarded in the life

Cure: Yellow bulb in the centre of the room and he has to wear a crystal necklace and peak himalayan mountain wall poster painting to be decorated or fixed on the south side corner wall and west side corner wall thereby creating a south west corner with mountains in his bedroom and office. Keep a green stone pyramid in the south west for strength & stability.

(C) Number 6 (representing metal) is missing in the chart which means he is missing friends or helpful people. He has struggled independently for his development in life or corner.

Cure: To wear a yellow metal bracelet on the hand or any yellow colour metal watch strap. Ladies will not have this problem as they wear golden bangles.

Hang a 5 rod yellow /golden wind chime in the N/W sector and place a pre-energised white or golden pyramid in NW.

Every human being is ruled by the direction influencing magnetic fields in his bedroom. According to the old testament both Indian and Chinese heritage the four main directions and the four cardinal directions give different energies to a person according to his /her date of birth or name , where the exact date of birth is not available. First we deal with the person having the birth date. Please use the following formula for determining the individual lucky numbers:-

Using the lunar calendar year of birth, add the two digits of the year till you get a single digit number e.g. A person born on 15 July,1943. In this case the lunar year according to Chinese numerology began on 5th Feb 1943. Now coming to the above birth date please take 1943 as the lunar year in this the last two digits i.e.4 and 3 are to be added to receive the single digit i.e.4+3=7.

Now the man deduct this number 7 from 10. The result number is 3, which is his lucky number. For women born on the above date add this two digit number with 5 i.e.4+3+5=12 (1+2=3) which is her lucky number.

Note:- If you get the number 10 adding the number then you have to consider 1+0=1. According to the table, know your directions.

The above person born with the lucky number 3 should keep his or her pillow in the south and east direction if they want total success or personal development. If they want to recover their health they must keep their pillow toward the North direction. If they want to get the children they must keep their pillow in the south- east direction. Similarly while working or studying the table they must face or visualise the above lucky directions. Thus this chart denotes the auspicious and inauspicious directions who know their date of birth. With the help of these three charts Laxmi Yantra, directionology and biorhythms one can easily obtain health, happiness, peace and prosperity in everyday life.

The table below can help you to fix the missing numbers in your Lo Shu grid.

Number	Direction	Element	Solution
1	North	Water	Put a water fountain or aquarium. Hang a painting or a picture of flowing water in a metal frame. Hang a light mirror or a wall clock.
2	Southwest	Big Earth	Hang a picture of mountains without water. Wear a necklace of pearls or crystals. Keep a pair of crystal balls, birds, or flowers. Keeping Amethyst/Rose quartz rocks or wearing a pendant. Bracelet with these stones will be very helpful in strengthening relationships. Keep a stone pyramid.
3	East	Wood	Keep an energized green stone pyramid. Put a small green plant or green bulb. Put a picture of greenery/green plants. Put a green octagonal pyramid. Keep a wooden pen, wooden key ring, etc. with you. Put a wooden wall clock on the East wall. (octagonal shape).
4	Southeast	Wood	Keep a picture of greenery. Keep an energized green stone pyramid. Light a green bulb, put up images of green trees. Keep an energized green pyramid in the Southeast direction of the bedroom. Keep a wooden pen, wooden key ring, etc with you.

5	Center	Earth	Hang high peak mountain poster without water. Wear a crystal pendant. Wear a pearl ring.s Keep a stone pyramid. Hang a yellow bulb in the centre of the room. Wear crystals in any form or shape. Hang a crystal chandelier or crystal balls.
6	Northwest	Metal	Wear a watch with a golden metallic chain. Hang 6 rod metal wind chime. Install energized white or metallic pyramid. Wear a yellow or golden armlet Wear a watch with a golden metal chain Put up a golden windchime with 6 rods. Keep a white or golden octagonal pyramid.
7	West	Metal	Wear a watch with a golden metallic chain. Hang 7 rod metallic wind chime. Install energized white or metallic pyramid. Wear a white silver armlet Wear a wrist watch with a silver metal chain Put up a silver wind chime with 7 rods. Keep a white or silver octagonal pyramid.

Matching the Elements to Energise

The easiest way to energize each particular sector is to match the element of that corner/direction with appropriate objects, shapes or colours and place them in that sector.

For the Southeast & East Use Plants

The southeast brings wealth and the east good family relationships and health. Choose healthy plants with broad succulent leaves representing the wood element. Blue carpets, wallpaper or pillows are also acceptable as they represent water, which symbolically “produces wood”.

For the Southwest, Northeast and Center Use Crystals

The southwest brings love and romance, the northeast good education luck and the center represents family luck. These three sectors are symbolic of the earth element...so place natural crystals in this area. Glass, pebbles, ceramics, granite ... things like this. Since fire produces earth in the 5 element cycle any item with red, or yellows and oranges are excellent for earth sectors.

For the North Use Water

Water features in the north bring career luck... but don't overdo it. Too much water is dangerous but in small doses brings enormous good fortune since water is also symbolic of money. Remember water should flow inward (never away from the home) and water features are not suitable in your bedroom even if it is in the north.

Instead energize the north sector of another room that you frequently use. Black or blue and white is an excellent colour combination to use in this area since white represents the metal element which supports water (blue or black).

For the South Use Lighting

The fire element in the south brings recognition, luck, respect and fame so bright lights and crystals here will energise this corner. A good colour combination is green and red - these work well from a feng shui perspective but if you feel these are too "Christmassy" then just tone down the shades - the colours don't have to be bright to energise the element!

For the West and Northwest Use Metal

The west represents children's luck and the northwest brings luck to the patriarch of the family as well as mentor luck. Windchimes are excellent here as they serve two purposes - they press down bad luck but also energise good luck! They move in the wind and their sounds create additional Yang energy. Shades of metallic colours, whites and golds are great here especially when combined with earth colours.

A word of caution: You can energise all sectors but a word of caution... don't over-energise any one sector by having too much of the particular element needed as this creates imbalance and can be dangerous.

Final Word

If you have come this far then by now some of you must have learnt something new and some of few must have some doubts and cynicism with the contradictory nature of the prediction method in the numerology. There are many instances where the prediction does not tally with the actual occurrence of the event in life. This is because of the freewill in action. With action and discipline one can shape their destiny but that destiny still lies under the limited contour created before the birth. Certain patterns always repeat in an individuals life irrespective of their success or failures and Astrology or Numerology makes you understand about those patterns in life.

Hope this book have managed to somewhat do the same for you.

Thank you

Printed by Libri Plureos GmbH in Hamburg, Germany